A French King
at
Holyrood

Front Cover

'Holyrood Palace and Chapel with Arthur's Seat and Salisbury Craggs'. Colour lithograph by S.D. Swarbreck, January, 1838 (*Private Collection, London*).

A French King at Holyrood

A. J. MACKENZIE-STUART

JOHN DONALD PUBLISHERS LTD
EDINBURGH

ISBN 0 85976 413 3

British Library Cataloguing in Publication Data
A catalogue record for this book is available from the British Library.

Phototypeset by WestKey Ltd, Falmouth, Cornwall
Printed & bound in Great Britain by Bell & Bain Ltd, Glasgow

Preface

More than thirty years ago I read a highly romanticised life of Louise de Polastron, badly translated from the French. It does not feature in the bibliography, though perhaps it should be given pride of place. I was on the point of abandoning it as intolerable when I came to the chapter on Louise's time in Edinburgh and immediately wondered how much of what I read was true; the present volume is the result of a quest pursued in the intervals of earning my living in another fashion.

The staff of the Edinburgh Room of Edinburgh City Libraries, helpful and courteous as ever, quickly provided me with *The Exiled Bourbons in Scotland* written by Francis Steuart, Advocate and man of letters, and published in 1908. I have gratefully quarried his book, although in almost every case I have gone back to the original sources, but, even in his own time, there was material already available in manuscript and in print about which Francis Steuart did not know. Since his day, there has also been published, particularly in France, much in the way of general history and relevant memoirs. This is the justification for what I now offer.

It has been decided that it would over-weight a book of this size and only distract the reader if it were to be equipped with a full apparatus of footnotes. I hope their absence is compensated by the reasonably complete bibliography which is appended.

I would like to thank the staff of the National Library of Scotland, the Scottish Record Office, the Scottish National Portrait Gallery, the Public Record Office at Kew, the Archives of the French Foreign Office and the Bibliothèque Méjane in Aix-en-Provence for their help and efficiency. I am also most grateful to the Duke of Buccleuch for allowing me to use the letters written by the duc d'Angoulême, which are among his family papers, and for letting me reproduce three of his paintings by Danloux. Mrs Dundas-Bekker of Arniston has also kindly let me use material from the Arniston letter books.

My warmest thanks go to the many friends who read all or part of this book in draft. I thank them for their patience and for their helpful comments.

The prize for patience must go to my wife who has nobly suffered this book's lengthy gestation and who has been my most valued critic. I only hope that she has to some extent been compensated by the pleasure we have both found in exploring the lesser known corners of France with which this book is concerned.

My final word of thanks goes to my old friend, William Prosser, who long ago suggested that this volume should be subtitled *Bourbons on the Rocks*.

Edinburgh, 1995 *A.J.M-S.*

Contents

Page

Chapter 1: Upbringing and Early Influences on the Comte d'Artois, 1757–96 1

Arrival at Leith on 6 January 1796 of the Comte d'Artois; procession to Holyrood; childhood and upbringing; his unsuccessful marriage; birth of his two sons, the Duc d'Angoulême and the Duc de Berry. The Versailles scene, its splendour and Artois's extravagant and dissolute behaviour. Examples, the building of the Château de Bagatelle in six weeks, and his simulated duel with the Duc de Bourbon; Artois and Louise de Polastron meet; the effect of Louise on his character and his devotion to her thereafter.

Chapter 2: Louise de Polastron 9

Louise de Polastron installed near Holyrood; her background and early years; her first meeting with Artois expanded; outbreak of the Revolution; ordered to leave France.

Chapter 3: Travels and the Offer of Asylum, 1789–96 15

Artois's travels (including a visit to Catherine the Great), whenever possible in the company of Louise, ending with his joining the Royalist forces at Coblenz; campaign of 1792 against France; the rout of Valmy; hardships; arrival in England and the ineffective expedition to the Ile d'Yeu; return to Portsmouth, where Artois finds himself unable to land because his creditors threaten imprisonment for debt. Decision of the British Government to offer the Palace of Holyroodhouse, both because it was a debtors' sanctuary, and because it was politically expedient to keep him at a safe distance from London.

Chapter 4: Early Days at the Palace of Holyrood 23

'Levees' and receptions which the great and good of Edinburgh attended. The gourmandising powers of the French. The arrival of the Duc d'Angoulême and other friends and courtiers; composition of the household; special reference to the arrival of a chaplain, the Abbé Latil, because of his increasing influence over Artois for the rest of his life; visits to the theatre; Angoulême goes hunting.

Chapter 5: Quality of Life at Holyroodhouse 35

Condition of the Palace at the time of Artois's arrival; the accommodation made available to Artois. Artois takes over further accommodation granted to Lord Adam Gordon; furniture of quality, provided by Trotters of Edinburgh, whose accounts are extant, and the substantial repairs and improvements—including waterclosets—which were made; lack of appreciation and understanding by modern French historians of level of comfort provided.

Chapter 6: Debtors and Sanctuary 43

The sanctuary of Holyrood; its origins and its extent on Artois's arrival. The history of imprisonment for debt in Scotland and how debtors could leave the sanctuary only on Sundays; the physical extent of the sanctuary, embracing the whole of the King's park and containing the debtors' village of St Ann's adjoining the palace; the life of the ordinary debtor.

Chapter 7: Comings and Goings of the Emigrés 49

More of the daily life of the émigrés; visits to Dalkeith House, domestic quarrels, sometimes with tragic results. A series of varied visitors: Danloux the painter, the Baron de Roll—an important if obscure figure in the royalist cause—and the Abbé Edgeworth, Louis XVI's confessor who accompanied him to the scaffold; the financial difficulty of the exiles. The chapter ends with a scene of amateur theatricals.

Chapter 8: The First Departure 59

The release of Artois from confinement, thanks to the Aliens Act, 1798, and his departure for London in August 1799. Further military activity impeded by 'an attack of haemorrhoids'.

Chapter 9: 'Tiresome and Odd'?:The Emigrés' View of the Scots 65

The attitudes of the émigrés, except for Capitaine de Boisgelin. Excerpts concerning visits, comments, the social round, are taken from his 1797 diaries preserved at Aix-en-Provence.

Chapter 10: Artois returns to the North, 1801 71

Return to Edinburgh at the end of 1801, due to his not being free from arrest for debt if a general peace with France should be concluded. This, the eventual Peace of Amiens, was regarded as highly likely. He remained, however, free to move around Scotland.

Chapter 11: Behind the Scenes in 1802 75

Comings and goings at Holyrood; meeting with the Orleans princes; Artois at the Hamilton races, with pen-portraits of Artois and the Duc de Berry by Lady Louisa Stuart and her cousin.

Chapter 12: A Napoleonic Spy in Edinburgh: The King goes back to London, 1803 81

Reports of spy activity in Edinburgh exist in the French Foreign Office and have been widely used. Among other things there is much careless talk of the plot on Napoleon's life being hatched in Edinburgh. The spy also mentions the death at Edinburgh of the elegant Agläé, Duchesse de Guiche (of burns caused by a fire in her room catching her clothing) and the insistence of the Abbé Latil that as she lay dying she should be separated from her lover. Artois and the Duc de Berry leave Edinburgh, and no record exists of their return until 1830. The chapter ends with a short comment on the possible identity of Napoleon's spy.

Chapter 13: The Death of Louise and the Renunciation of Holyroodhouse 89

The disastrous outcome of the conspiracy against Napoleon which had been plotted in Edinburgh; arrest and execution or imprisonment of the conspirators. The death, in 1804, of Louise de Polastron and the increasing dominance over Artois of the Abbé, later Cardinal, Latil. Meanwhile a few *émigrés* remain at Holyrood; the palace is increasingly put on a care and maintenance basis; defeat of Napoleon sees the last of the French depart.

Chapter 14: Events in France, 1814–30 99

This chapter summarises the events in France over a sixteen-year period and tries to explain the reasons why Artois, now Charles X of France, was forced to abdicate by the Revolution of 1830; contemporary memoirs describe the changed attitude of the former *émigrés* to their Scottish hosts. In England, Charles X is threatened by his creditors and once again he is offered asylum at Holyrood.

Chapter 15: Charles Arrives at Newhaven: Re-established at Holyrood 107

His greeting on arrival, and the hostile attitude, in part, of the Scottish press, and Sir Walter Scott's reply; the dilapidated state of Holyrood; the Duc and Duchesse of Angoulême install themselves in Regent Terrace; problems over the regency of France after Charles's abdication; arrival of Charles's tempestuous daughter-in-law, the Duchesse de Berry, also installed in Regent Terrace, and her intention to instigate a rising in France; Charles's financial troubles; carriages are arrested for debt and action raised against him in the Court of Session—an action only settled after his death; changed religious climate; the new Catholic cathedral in Edinburgh and the part played by Charles in furthering the Catholic cause.

Chapter 16: More Perambulations of the King and the Comments of Edinburgh 117

The domestic round at Holyrood; his outings and the reaction of Edinburgh society; the education of his grandson, the Duc de Bordeaux, and what he was taken to see; lease of Baberton House; the friends made by his chief aide, the Baron de Damas; the education and friends of Charles's grand-daughter, Louise, and her character and experiences.

Chapter 17: Varied Impressions: Last Days in Edinburgh and Departure for Prague, 1832 127

The tide turns against Charles X; the reasons explained; visitors to Edinburgh and their impressions; decision to seek the aid of the Austrian Emperor; an offer of part of the vast Hradschin Palace at Prague is made; extended and warm-hearted ceremonies of departure; Charles X's departure by chartered merchant ship to Rotterdam, since the Government ship promised had not arrived; uncaring attitude of British Government and the Duke of Wellington's reactions.

Epilogue: The Final Phase—Death of Charles in 1836 135

Life at Prague; the comings and goings of the few old friends left. Once again, Charles is required to move; cholera epidemic and his eventual death at Goritz, now just inside Slovenia, over the Italian frontier, in 1836.

Sources and Bibliography 138

CHAPTER 1

Upbringing and Early Influences on the Comte d'Artois, 1757–96

On the morning of Wednesday, 6 January 1796, the frigate *Jason* dropped anchor in Leith Roads to the accompaniment of a salute of twenty-one guns from the battery at Leith Fort. She carried as her principal passenger 'Monsieur', His Royal Highness Charles-Philippe, the Comte d'Artois, youngest brother of the late King of France, Louis XVI. Artois's destination was the Palace of Holyroodhouse and the debtors' sanctuary of which it was the heart and of which he had pressing need. For nearly three years the palace became not only Artois's refuge but his prison, and for three years more it remained his home and headquarters. Once again, 35 years later and in the wake of the July Revolution of 1830, Artois, by then Charles X, the last Bourbon king of France and Navarre, sought refuge in Holyrood and lived there for two years. The purpose of this book is to give some account of these almost forgotten eddies created by the current of events in Europe.

Modern French historians have, for the most part, created their own romantic myth to describe the arrival of Artois in Scotland. To give only one example, Lucas-Dubreton, writing in 1927: 'One night he was landed on the coast near Leith and, thanks to the connivance of the British Cabinet, was whisked in secrecy to Holyrood in the surroundings of Edinburgh.'

Secrecy is a comparative term. It is true that, as reported in the *Edinburgh Advertiser*, Artois wished 'as little ceremony as possible' and the Windsor Foresters and Hopetoun Fencibles, who were to have lined the route to the palace, were told to stand down, no doubt with characteristic military comment on the unnecessary application of pipe-clay and metal polish. For the rest, the landing could scarcely have been more of a public occasion. At two o'clock that afternoon, when Artois set foot on shore, a further salute of twenty-one guns greeted him with yet another from the castle when at last his procession reached Holyroodhouse. At the pier of Leith were Lord Adam Gordon, Commander-in-Chief of the forces of North Britain, and his staff. Half the population of Edinburgh turned out to witness the spectacle. As the *Gentleman's Magazine* for that month put it, 'The crowd of people on the quay, and all the way from it to the Palace, was extraordinary; beside, every window was fitted, and the joy expressed on His Royal Highness's safe arrival in Scotland seemed very general.'

The crowd was well rewarded. That acute observer, Pryse Lockhart Gordon, perhaps better known for his description of Brussels on the eve of Waterloo, had a close-up view.

> I was at this time aide-de-camp to General Drummond of Strathallan and we headed the cavalcade, the adjutant and quarter-master General with his Lordship's staff bringing up the rear; his excellency [Lord Adam Gordon] in his coach, painted black, with four long-tailed sable horses at the centre. Nothing could be more lugubrious than this procession. The Duchess of Athol, spouse to the noble Lord, had lately died, which was the cause of this sombre equipage. Their Royal Highnesses [sic] occupied the coach, carriages having been provided for their retinue.

The journey was not without drama:

> A great crowd had assembled, especially on the north bridge where there was a halt. I was sent to ascertain the cause, and found that a horse in a coal cart had dropped down and expired. So great was the crowd that it was with difficulty this obstruction could be removed, and it was considered a bad omen by the strangers.

So it was that Artois's first exile in Scotland began.

Charles-Philippe, Comte d'Artois, was born on 7 October 1757, the youngest of the three surviving sons of the Grand Dauphin, the only son of Louis XV. The eldest, the Duc de Berry, became Louis XVI, and the next, the Comte de Provence, became Louis XVIII. Had the Grand Dauphin lived to succeed his father the history of the French monarchy might have been very different. Austere, devout and conscientious, he stood apart from the strange mixture of pomp and frivolity that was characteristic of Versailles. He died, however, when Charles-Philippe was aged eight, followed by his wife some two years later. With the death of his parents the last opportunity of educating the young prince vanished. In accordance with custom, Artois and his brothers had their own household presided over by their Governor, the Duc de la Vauguyon. The latter was a gallant and successful general but was more interested in preserving his position at court, with all the perquisites attaching to it, than in instructing his charges. From his own point of view he succeeded admirably since he died in office. Vauguyon made no inconvenient demands upon Louis XV and let the princes do what they wished. With Artois's elder brothers—the eldest, the Duc de Bourgogne, had died in infancy—this policy was less disastrous than it might have been, although in later life the Duc de Berry, the future Louis XVI, cherished the utmost distaste for his mentor. In the case of Louis XVI and in that of his next brother, the Comte de Provence, enough natural aptitude remained for their education to progress beyond formal limits. Artois, however, was endowed with no such stimulus. Early reports speak of his cheerful frankness, happy irresponsibility and spontaneous generosity—qualities which remained with him for a large part of his life; admirable qualities, no doubt, but insufficient to serve him well when later he was called upon to exercise judgement in circumstances of great difficulty.

If Artois had been allowed to become a soldier matters might have been otherwise, although the direct line of the Bourbons had no martial tradition and their lack of enthusiasm for command in the field was no doubt wisely encouraged by their generals. Triumphal entries were another matter, as the number of arches and obelisks attesting the arrival of Louis XIV and Louis XV, scattered throughout France, amply demonstrate. Artois, it is true, was, at the age of fifteen, given the position of Colonel-General of the Swiss Guards, but this office was decorative only and one in which it was difficult to make a serious mistake. Artois, nonetheless, managed to do so. Common sense dictated that a visit to the Ecole Militaire should be made in uniform and on horseback. Artois arrived dressed in apple-green, shot with gold and silver thread, and carrying a ridiculous plumed hat beneath his arm. Worse still, he arrived on foot. Even this innocuous pastime of playing at soldiers, however, was discouraged. The Comte de Maurepas, then in charge of the royal finances, is quoted as saying, 'You find yourself much attracted by manoeuvres, Monseigneur? That is not a suitable occupation for a prince. Find yourself something else to do. Run up debts and we will pay them.' A contemporary moralist said of the young princes, 'The guardianship in which they were held left them no road open except that which led them to vice.' Artois was only too ready to follow the signpost. His natural good looks and cheerfulness, coupled with his unwillingness to concentrate on any serious object, made superfluous the advice which Maurepas had given him.

After the death of the Duc de la Vauguyon Artois accordingly settled down to a routine of extravagance and scandal on a scale only made possible by his rank and position. One duty and one duty alone was his, that of marriage, and at the age of sixteen he was betrothed to Marie-Thérèse of Savoy, daughter of the King of Sardinia and the younger sister of Marie-Josephine who had earlier married Artois's elder brother the Comte de Provence, the future Louis XVIII. The marriage between Artois and Marie-Thérèse took place in the chapel of Versailles on 16 November 1773.

It was in every way a disastrous marriage even by the standards of the time, although that of the Comte de Provence ran it very close. To judge from the indifferent portraits which survive, Marie-Thérèse had a certain simple prettiness but this was not enough to see her over the hurdles of etiquette which Versailles raised in the path of the unwary stranger. One can only have pity for her. Until her marriage she had been reared in the strict, almost monastic, surroundings of the Court of Turin. Her timidity, her gaucheness, her dislike of worldly pleasure made her the most inappropriate companion for her husband. Despite the kindness and protection of Marie-Antoinette, she failed completely to make her mark at Court, and having done her duty by producing two sons, the Duc d'Angoulême in 1775 and the Duc de Berry in 1778, she retired from Versailles to St Cloud and almost retires from this story. Many years later she died in Austria, at Gratz, and was buried under her maiden name without mention of her marriage.

It cannot be said that Artois showed any greater sense of responsibility in dealing with his own children than he showed in any other direction. The Duc d'Angoulême and the Duc de Berry were confined to the care of the Duc de Sérent, who supervised their independent establishment at the Chateau de Beauregard, not far from Marly, where, as the Duc d'Angoulême was to say in later life, 'we were brought up like pigs.' The Duc de Sérent and his son we shall meet again at Holyrood.

When his grandfather, Louis XV, died in 1775, the final restraint on Artois disappeared. Henceforth he was to be the prime mover in the circle which formed around Marie-Antoinette and which was to provoke so much public animosity as the years went by. Artois had every privilege and no obligations. His quarters were the whole of the first floor of the Orangerie wing of the Palace of Versailles. The Orangerie itself was one of the finest in Europe, where, even in the cold of winter, it was possible to stroll in the heady scent of orange blossom. The furnishings of Artois's apartments were superb, the best that the greatest *ébénistes* and *ciseleurs* of Paris could achieve. In these magnificent surroundings there were constant parties, suppers which lasted through the night and, above all, gambling, a passion which Artois shared with his sister-in-law, the Queen. Louis XVI did what he could to abate this scourge which not only ruined scores of his courtiers but was bringing the entire court into public contempt. Within a year of Louis XVI's ascending the throne Marie-Antoinette had become indebted to the extent of no less than 487,000 livres. The King, as ever, paid. There is a well-known story of how Louis XVI, in an attempt to restrict the Queen's card-playing, extracted a promise from her that on a visit she was making she would only play one game of faro. The promise was honoured but the game lasted thirty-six hours without stop. Not that charity was wholly neglected. Each evening one of the two Curés of Versailles stood in attendance at the entry of the salon where gambling was in progress and a purse would be handed in for the poor. Perhaps 50 or a 100 louis would be collected in an evening where 100,000 were changing hands across the tables.

Thomas Carlyle, half a century later, describes the scene with justifiable invective:

> The grand events are but a charitable Feast of Morals, with their Prizes and Speeches; Poissarde Processions to the Dauphin's cradle; above all, Flirtations, their rise, progress, decline and fall. There are Snow-statues raised by the poor in hard winter to a Queen who has given them fuel. There are masquerades, theatricals; beautifyings of Little Trianon, purchase and repair of St. Cloud; journeyings from the summer Court-Elysium to the winter one . . . Wholly the lightest-hearted frivolous foam of Existence; yet an artfully refined foam; pleasant were it not so costly, like that which mantles on the wine of Champagne.

Artois is not spared by the Sage of Chelsea.

> Monseigneur d'Artois pulls the mask from a fair impertinent, fights a duel in consequence—almost to drawing blood. He has breeches of a kind new in this world—a fabulous kind; 'four tall lackeys', says Mercier, as if he had seen it, 'hold him up in the air, that he may fall into the garment without vestige of wrinkle; from which rigorous encasement the same four, in the same way, and with more effort, have to deliver him at night.'

Artois did not confine his activities to Versailles. Until his meeting with Louise de Polastron, of which more later, he frequented the theatres and little houses of Paris. In this respect he was a typical Bourbon who in sexual matters seldom did things by half. Either, like Louis XV, they behaved like stags in the rutting season or, like Louis XVI, they were for practical purposes celibate. There is no point in rehearsing the catalogue of Artois's conquests, if conquest is the appropriate term when the conqueror is a prince of the blood royal and possessed, if not of vast wealth, at least of vast credit and when those who are conquered are primarily interested in what that credit can obtain.

As his Paris base Artois had the Palais du Temple, the former priory of the Order of St John of Jerusalem. His elder son, the Duc d'Angoulême, had, at the age of one, been appointed its Grand Prior. Portraits of the young Angoulême show him wearing the Maltese cross of his office, and Artois had no hesitation in using the Order's property as his own. This he proceeded to furnish *à la Turque*, with tented ceilings and draped, curvaceous furniture.

Two incidents will serve to illustrate the character of Artois at this period. The first was the building of Bagatelle. During the summer of 1776 the Royal Family was about to make one of its visits to Fontainebleau. Before setting out Artois wagered with the Queen a sum of 100,000 francs that on her return he would entertain her in a chateau in the Bois de Boulogne which he would have built in the space of six weeks. This was just the sort of wager to enchant Marie-Antoinette and the bet was on. Eight hundred workers were employed night and day, and Béllanger's bewitching building, where fifty years later the Marquess of Hereford was to gather again so many of the treasures scattered by the Revolution, rose like magic from the ground. On her return the Queen went to see whether Artois had indeed won his bet. Not only was the chateau completed but the grounds had been laid out with the utmost skill; the English garden, the Chinese garden, the terrace lined with statues which led to the principal entrance over which was carved the motto *parva sed apta*. Upstairs, Artois's bedroom paid tribute to the martial qualities he so conspicuously lacked. Trophies and fasces abounded and, above the bed, wall coverings imitated the folds of a tent. It is not to be supposed, however, that the Queen saw all the decoration. One room, at least, was embellished with frescoes and high-relief in imitation of the more explicit wall-paintings recently uncovered at Herculaneum.

The cost of all this was, of course, immense. Calonne, the Finance Minister, is reported to have said that Artois cost the Royal Treasury even more than the Queen herself. The King tried in vain to induce some spirit of moderation in his youngest brother but neither private remonstration nor public rebuke had the slightest effect in curbing Artois's expenditure or in checking his personal behaviour.

The second episode, already foreshadowed in the quotation from Carlyle, exemplifies the latter.

On Shrove Tuesday, 1778, there was a masked ball at the Opera. Artois was there, accompanied by Madame de Canillac. Together they met the Duchesse de Bourbon, born an Orléans and daughter-in-law of the powerful Prince de Condé. The Duchesse disliked Madame de Canillac intensely for the good reason that when the latter had been her lady-in-waiting she had also been the mistress of her husband. There was an exchange of bitter-sweet remarks. Artois, who was slightly drunk, pretended that the Duchesse was one of the professional habituées of the Opera and proceeded to ask her price. 'It could only be Monsieur d'Artois or a scoundrel who could speak to me like that,' replied the Duchesse, seizing the mask which Artois was wearing. Artois in his turn snatched her mask from the Duchesse, scraped her face and, taking advantage of the general consternation, disappeared into the crowd. That evening he boasted of what he had done in the salon of the Polignac family at Versailles. In her turn the Duchesse de Bourbon publicly declared that Artois was the most insolent of men and that she had thought of calling the guard to have him arrested. At last, her father-in-law, the Prince de Condé, demanded that the King should intervene. Louis XVI ordered that amity should be restored without further discussion but Artois only enraged further the Duc de Bourbon and the Duchesse demanded that her husband challenge Artois to a duel. Both participants were more than reluctant, the Duc de Bourbon because he did not wish to commit the enormous crime of wounding the King's brother; Artois because personal valour was not his strongest suit. After a few minutes' sword-play in the Bois de Boulogne they each surrendered to the other without either giving or receiving a scratch. The news soon spread through Paris. Courage might have raised Artois in the eyes of the mob; its lack lowered him still further.

The Bastille fell in July 1789, and in the mistaken and myopic hope that the gathering forces of revolution might thus be diverted, Louis XVI ordered Artois to leave France. Since then Artois had lived the life of an *émigré* seeking hospitality and support where they could be be found among the Courts of Europe. Some account of his wanderings follows in a later chapter. In January 1796, however, for the first time in six years, he had the prospect of a settled home under the leaking roof of Holyroodhouse.

Nonetheless, by the time Artois landed at the pier of Leith he was, in one respect, a much changed man. For more than a decade before his arrival in Scotland his affections had become centred on one person, Louise d'Esparbès, Comtesse de Polastron. In a letter written in 1785 to their mutual friend Madame de Lage, Artois could say in all sincerity, 'In the whole universe I exist for her alone.'

For the moment, then, we leave the funereal cortège on its journey from Leith, clattering down the narrow and insanitary Canongate—which must have recalled to Artois the Marais in Paris where he had his *hôtel privé*—and introduce Madame de Polastron.

CHAPTER 2

Louise de Polastron

'While the Comte resided in Holyrood House, his mistress, Madame Polistron, lived in a small white-washed house, at the entry to Croftanrigh looking into the park.' So wrote Robert Chambers in his *Walks in Edinburgh* published in 1825. Elsewhere he describes the house as standing 'on the left of the Chapel looking into the park'. Croft-an-Righ means the 'The King's Field' and is today a short cul-de-sac leading from Abbeyhill to the northern boundary of the Palace gardens and which originally gave access to the Abbey churchyard. Today the only building of interest which remains is a house, perhaps of sixteenth century origin, but much rebuilt in the seventeenth century, popularly known as Regent Moray's House and so known when Artois's followers began to gather in Edinburgh. Regent Moray's House is too big to answer to the description given by Robert Chambers, although it is situated at the south-western end of Croft-an-Righ and could reasonably be characterised as 'looking into the park.' Although in 1796 Croft-an-Righ was much more built up than it is now, the enclosure opposite Regent Moray's House was and still is garden ground.

Maps of the period, however, show a small house abutting on the grounds of Holyrood immediately to the south of Regent Moray's House. To the observer facing east it would be the building immediately to the left of the Chapel. On the earliest large-scale Ordnance Survey this is called St. Anne's Lodge and it is probably here that Louise de Polastron was installed. The name is explained by the neighbouring house of the Abbot of Holyrood which stood by the west door of the Abbey Church until well into the nineteenth century and which had a chapel dedicated to St. Anne. Its position also ties in with the report of a spy sent by Napoleon to Edinburgh in 1803, that Louise lived in 'a small but independent house not more than ten paces from the Palace'.

Louise de Polastron was born in Paris on 19 October 1764. Her father was the Comte d'Esparbès de Lussan, *maréchal des champs et armées du roi*, and her mother was Marie-Catherine Julie Rougeot, a daughter of Claude-Francois Rougeot, the hereditary *receveur général* of the

Domains of Burgundy, and immensely rich. Louise de Polastron both had her cake and was able to eat it. On her father's side she inherited lineage and distinction; on her mother's she inherited money. Her mother died, however, when Louise was only six weeks old and her father soon remarried. Fortunately, Louise remained on excellent terms with her father and her half brother and sisters and she paid many childhood visits to her de Lussan uncle at the elegant Château de La Motte-Bardigue. The chateau still remains, caught in the web of time, in the gentle countryside of Montauban. Nonetheless, it was Rougeot, her financier grandfather, who supervised her upbringing.

Louise was educated at the Royal Abbey of Panthément which had moved to Paris in 1771. Much of the building can be found today at the corner of the rue de Grenelle and the rue de Bellechasse, somewhat improbably occupied by the Ministry of War Pensions. As is common with monastic buildings in France it has served its turn as barracks and a prison, and it is difficult now to picture it as it was, a *grand isle de verdure* in the heart of the faubourg St Germain, its gardens blending with those of the convent of Bellechasse which adjoined. The rococo chapel remains undisturbed, although now used as a Protestant church and although access is only possible through an unprepossessing alley.

From her cramped quarters in St Anne's Lodge Louise de Polastron looked back with nostalgia upon her time at Panthémont. It is easy to sense the emotion she felt when, although only 34, consumptive, and her eyesight failing, she received at Holyrood the following letter from her old friend and contemporary at the Abbey of Panthémont, 'Blimonette', Stephanie-Beatrix d'Amblimont, Marquise de Lage de Volude, then in Madrid.

> How I laughed at your disquisition on the subject of your spectacles! . . . When I look back to the day of our first communion, twenty years, one month and seven days ago, I see you at my side, in the middle of the choir at Panthémont, your elegant figure, your charming face and your open and tranquil manner; I think of our general confession and our childhood, of all the time that we had before us and a future which was so happy in the beginning and so stormy thereafter . . .
>
> I spend my days recalling these pictures of my old and dear friends . . . from 1 November 1778 to 1 November 1798 is all our life. I could be a grandmother and you wear spectacles.

Panthémont was an abbey only in name. The Abbess was always chosen from the nobility and the pupils included many of the princesses from the younger Bourbon line. In theory a conventual rule was followed but, as one author has put it, its demands 'knew how to yield before necessary indulgence and to excuse the caprices or inattention of future duchesses.'

One such was Yolande de Polastron, the future Duchesse de Polignac. It was on a return visit to Panthémont, where she herself had been educated, that she and Louise met. Yolande was captivated by Louise, *la tendresse vivante* as Lamartine described her, and so strong was the spell that she approached Louise's father with the suggestion that her half-brother, the Vicomte Adhémar de Polastron, was a suitable candidate for Louise's hand in marriage. Louise was young and could expect a large dowry. While she could well have waited it seemed to her father an opportunity not to be missed. Not only was the Polastron pedigree documented over seven centuries, there was the bond with Madame de Polignac. The Polignac family were already well established at court but, more pertinently, it was Marie-Antoinette's habit to have at any given time a particular *confidante*. The day of Yolande de Polignac was about to dawn

The marriage between Louise d'Esparbes and Adhémar de Polastron took place at Versailles on 5 June 1780. The marriage contract was signed by the King and Queen and, significantly enough in the light of future events, by Artois.

Louise was just over fifteen and her husband only a few months past his eighteenth birthday. Following precedent it was decided that the parties were as yet too young to live together and once the nuptial pomp and circumstance had been observed Louise was returned to Panthémont, marriage, apparently, being no bar to her continued residence, and Adhémar de Polastron rejoined his regiment at Strasbourg. It was feared that he might follow the royal precedent of the Duc de Bourbon, he of the duel with Artois, who, under a similar restriction, so successfully eloped with his young wife that further separation was valueless.

It seems fairly certain that Adhémar initially acquiesced in the enforced separation with becoming reluctance but when it ended it was plain that the marriage was one of form only save for the necessary prelude to the birth of a son, Anne-Louis-Henri de Polastron, in October 1785. Adhémar de Polastron, unlike his sister and his wife, had no taste for Versailles and his naturally morose character found comfort only in the life of a soldier and in playing his violin. At the same time he deserves more compassion than he has generally received. The velvet jungle of the court was not the paradise its devotees imagined it to be; the world of camp and barrack might be brutalising but it was at least closer to reality. Moreover, after the Revolution, he served the Royalist cause well and was ill rewarded, dying poor in 1821 in a garrison post at Bayonne, although Artois, to his credit, took care of his widowed second wife.

For Louise, however, all was gold, and it is the glitter of Versailles seen against the sombre surroundings of Holyrood, Victor Hugo's '*Chateau decouronne! Vallée expiatoire!*'—'Chateau without a crown! Valley of atonement!'—which provides the antithesis essential to true romantic art. This narrative, however, primarily concerns the valley of atonement and it is necessary to be selective in making the contrast between Holyrood and the magnificence of Versailles. As with Artois, two images must suffice to represent a decade of brittle and brilliant make-believe.

The first is a letter by grandfather Rougeot to Louise's uncle, the Comte d'Esparbès, in which one can feel the bemused delight of the old financier at his grand-daughter's forthcoming official presentation at Court. Agläe de Guiche, Yolande de Polignac's daughter, was similarly to be presented the following week.

> There is to be new costume for the presentation and it is your niece and Madame de Guiche who are to set the fashion. The Queen wishes to revive the old form with its splendour and brilliance and that, it is said, on the representations of the trade to the profit of those who manufacture velvet and cloth of gold and who are likely to fail if the Court does not come to their aid. Thus it has been decreed that your niece will be presented in the most formal manner, the body of the dress being black velvet, the skirt in cloth of gold, as will be the scarf and belt. All this will be covered in diamonds belonging to the Queen and to the Comtesse d'Artois who have had the kindness to lend them to her as they have to Madame de Guiche who will be presented a week after. Madame de Polignac has, as her wedding present, made a gift to your niece of her dresses both for the Versailles presentation and for the presentation to the Royal Princes.

The second illustration is the famous engraving by de Launay, *Le Chiffre d'Amour*, after Fragonard's painting in the Wallace Collection.

In profile, the arch of her neck and the flow of her skirt forming a graceful arabesque, a Court beauty carves the initials of her lover on a tree. The branches of the tree echo the same curves and blend into an idyllic landscape beyond. A letter from the lover lies on the ground beside a stone bench where it has been read and re-read throughout the endless summer afternoon. Not even the immobile dog patiently watching his mistress disturbs the serenity. It is unlikely that Louise was the model for

Fragonard's painting, but the engraving is dedicated to 'Madame la Vicomtesse de Polastron, Dame du Palais', and by its association with Louise epitomises the stillness which she knew, endless in prospect and so brief in fact, before the breaking storm.

Artois is sometimes credited—if that be the correct word to use—with the paternity of Louis de Polastron. The most recent biographer of Louise de Polastron, Monique de Heurtas, is adamant that this was not the case. She stresses the absence of any recorded avowal by Artois to his close friend the Comte de Vaudreuil or any complaint by the Comtesse d'Artois. Neither reason is very convincing. Vaudreuil was in attendance at Versailles; no letter was needed for a confidence. The Comtesse was hardened to her husband's extra-mural activities. It is also suggested that Artois never subsequently showed any special regard for Louis, but given all the circumstances of the emigration it is difficult to see what more he could have done. The matter remains open. The best argument against Artois's paternity is that it was only after the birth of Louis that Artois is reported as assiduous in the attentions he paid to Louise. Nonetheless it was only a matter of months after the birth of Louis in 1785 before Louise was openly recognised as the mistress of Artois. Nothing remarkable about that viewed against the quadrille of Versailles liaisons. What was exceptional was the depth of their mutual devotion, a devotion that never diminished, in good times and bad, until the death of Louise in London in 1804. Through all the tribulations of the emigration she remained his loyal and adoring companion; Artois, for his part, despite her failing looks and health, stayed constant to the end. In his letters written in exile to his oldest and closest friend, the Comte de Vaudreuil, we find the well-being of his *chère amie* his first concern. Indeed Artois's detractors maintained that he put the care of his mistress before his duties as a prince, while Louise, for her part, dissuaded him from exposure to danger, and there is at least some truth in this charge.

Once Artois had begun to concentrate his attentions upon Louise de Polastron his former debauched life came to an end and it became necessary for him to find some other outlet for his surplus energy. Although devoid of any political experience and wisdom, it was to politics that he turned. Given his temperament and his upbringing there was only one position that could attract him. It was as a champion of the monarchy that Artois appeared; monarchy beyond compromise, monarchy at its most absolute. Any diminution of the royal prerogative was unthinkable. Unfortunately, in the affairs of state, as in his own private affairs, Artois was incapable of understanding the most elementary economic laws. He firmly believed that the expenses of the monarchy could not be regulated by its receipts but that, on the contrary, receipts must be regulated by expenditure. This is not a good maxim at the best of times and at this stage of the eighteenth century France was almost bankrupt.

Artois's intransigent attitude alarmed both the King and the Queen. Louis XVI, for his part, was ready to make some concession to public opinion, although he was never able to decide what form that concession should take. Even Marie-Antoinette, who a few years before would have shared Artois's attitude wholeheartedly, had become a frightened woman. Artois, however, did not lack supporters. Around him there formed a group of those courtiers who saw in the continuance of life at Versailles as they knew it the only guarantee of their personal prosperity. Thus, Artois became the leader of a party of the right and as their head the particular target for all forms of popular discontent. Day by day his unpopularity grew. His appearances were marked by catcalls and jeers from the people. Old scandals were recalled and what had once amused the mob now aroused its anger. To the more enlightened politicians he was the subject of distrust and dislike. During the critical summer of 1789 it was Artois, not the King, who was the focus of mounting resentment.

During the night of 14 July 1789, the Master of the Royal Wardrobe, the Duc de La Rochefoucault-Liancourt awoke the King with the news that the Bastille had fallen and there followed the famous exchange—'It is a revolt?'—'No, sire, it is a revolution.' By now a price had been put upon the head of Artois and Louis XVI decided that in the departure of his brother lay the only hope for the monarchy.

On 16 July 1789 Artois's odyssey began. Accompanied by the Comte de Vaudreuil and a handful of his entourage he reached Valenciennes where he was joined by the Duc de Sérent, bringing with him Artois's sons, the Duc D'Angoulême and the Duc de Berry. On 19 July he entered Brussels where the Prince de Condé and his two sons awaited him. So began the convoluted journey which six years later was to lead him to the Palace of Holyroodhouse. 'We shall be back in three months,' said Artois on leaving Versailles. He was wrong by a quarter of a century.

CHAPTER 3

Travels and the Offer of Asylum, 1789–96

Artois's travels between 1789 and his arrival in Scotland in 1796 covered much of Europe. They were tragic years for the French monarchy. The Royalist army based on Germany was destroyed in 1792; Louis XVI and Marie-Antoinette were executed in 1793 and Robespierre's murderous campaign of 'purification' was initiated.

After his re-union with his sons and the Duc de Sérent in Valenciennes, Artois journeyed south. To his great joy Louise de Polastron joined him in Switzerland, where, some two miles from Berne, they passed an idyllic fortnight. By easy stages he reached, in September 1789, the court of his father-in-law, the King of Sardinia, at Turin. On the surface the meeting was wholly amicable but after a short interval relations became strained. The King resented the continual drain on his purse which Artois and his, by then, numerous followers provoked. More serious, however, was the arrival in October of Louise, shortly after the arrival of the Comtesse d'Artois herself. The King was outraged and Louise betook herself to Rome in company with the Comte de Vaudreuil and the rest of the Polignac clan.

In a letter dated 5 December 1789 the Comte de Vaudreuil wrote to Artois, 'Your existence is the safeguard of the Royal Family and of the Monarchy.' Untrue as this was Artois was only too ready to believe it and the consequences were grave. Artois could have done comparatively little harm to his eldest brother if he had continued to batten upon his father-in-law, but, unhappily, his absolutist principles and the military enthusiasm of the Prince de Condé spurred him to action. This took the form of soliciting aid from the other powers with the object of restoring the Bourbons by force. Such conduct ran counter to the policy of Louis XVI and, indeed, was contrary to his direct orders. Louis XVI, who by now was virtually a prisoner in the Tuileries, realised that the only hope for the survival of the monarchy, both in his own person and as an institution, lay in persuading the people of France that his patriotism was beyond reproach. To bolster his position by seeking foreign aid and foreign arms would, in the eyes of the Constituent Assembly, be a betrayal of France.

Early in 1791 Artois sought an interview in Vienna with the Emperor, the brother of Marie-Antoinette. The Emperor, no doubt well warned by his sister, refused such a meeting and the only positive gain which Artois obtained was a protracted *dolce far niente* with his beloved Louise in Venice. On his return to Turin it was borne in upon Artois that he had outstayed his welcome. He looked for a base nearer France and he and his entourage moved to Coblenz where he was welcomed by the Elector of Trier, Clement-Wenceslas. Whether the welcome would have been quite so enthusiastic if the Elector had realised that his town was to become for the next two years a French city and the *émigré* capital is more questionable.

There, in the houses put at his disposal by the obliging Elector, Artois re-established a semblance of the past glories of Versailles and for a brief moment it appeared as if the fortunes of the *émigrés* were taking an upward turn. In August 1791 there was a meeting between Artois, the Emperor and the King of Prussia. Artois was received with honour and, soon after, Austria and Prussia promulgated the Declaration of Pilnitz, by which they agreed to intervene in the affairs of France should such an intervention be resolved by all the powers of Europe. Artois was triumphant. Inevitably, however, frictions arose and factions developed. Artois's brother, the Comte de Provence, the only other member of the Royal Family to make his way abroad after the abortive flight of Louis XVI and Marie-Antoinette to Varennes, considered that the policy which Artois had been pursuing in Italy only endangered the King and Queen. Artois, in turn, regarded the attitude of the Comte de Provence as little less than pandering to the Revolution. Both in turn were suspicious of those *émigrés* who looked for their instructions only to the imprisoned King of France, since those instructions, they maintained, were given under duress.

In March 1792, Austria, at last, declared war upon France and, for the first time for many months, the *émigrés* were united in their enthusiasm at the prospect of immediate action and a return to their own country.

In August the march began. The invading army comprised Prussian, Austrian and French *émigré* troops. Divisions had already emerged over the role which each contingent was to play. Provence and Artois commanded the French *Armée des Princes*. Numerically small in comparison with the other elements, it nonetheless provided an astonishing spectacle. It was as if some Gobelins tapestry had come to life, a tapestry designed by Oudry in glorification of Louis XV's mania for the hunt. There were companies composed entirely of officers, swarms of aides-de-camp surrounding the Princes, troops of valets and fanfares of hunting horns, and baggage train on baggage train, because no gentleman could go to war unless suitably provided with all the comforts necessary to mitigate the rigours of a campaign in the field. The comforts, of course, included camp followers, if such a term may be used for the ageing Princesse de Monaco, the mistress of the Prince de Condé. On the other hand, essentials such as arms and adequate rations for the troops were miserably lacking.

Whether for reasons of national prejudice or military wisdom the *émigré* forces were never actively engaged in battle, but they shared to the full the total rout, in torrential rain, which followed the Republican victories of Valmy and Jemappes in September and November 1792. Not for the last time Flanders mud took its toll.

The Prussians and Austrians fared badly, but for the French exiles the disaster was total. A national army can at least hope to return to base and lick its wounds in its native villages. For the exiles there was no native village to receive them. Split into small groups they were left to forage as best they could across the whole of Eastern Europe. Some units were more fortunate than others and found protection and support as mercenaries in the pay of Russia and other powers.

For Artois the defeat was doubly tragic. After the Indian Summer of Coblenz he found himself pursued on all sides for the debts which he had incurred in equipping, however ineffectively, the *émigré* army. We can only speculate upon the true amount of those debts. Vaudreuil, writing to a cousin a couple of years later, maintained that they were less than 80,000 or 90,000 pounds sterling. 'I have seen the accounts. What is this modest sum in comparison with the thousands so ill-spent by England? It is a drop in the ocean when added to the torrent of gold poured out by the British Cabinet.' Whatever the amount, these debts were to beset Artois for the remainder of his life. He was arrested by one creditor at Aachen and only with the greatest difficulty was he able to reach the gloomy neighbourhood of Hamm in Westphalia and there to join the Comte de Provence.

The year 1793 was scarcely more successful. After the execution of Louis XVI in January the French crown had devolved upon his young son, the 'Orphan of the Temple', who in legitimist eyes became Louis XVII. Artois, inevitably, was stricken by grief. As late as the beginning of January 1793 he is writing, optimistically, to his friend the Comte de Vaudreuil, 'The latest news is more reassuring and the firmness with which [Louis XVI] has replied to his two questionnaires has made a great impression on the people.' By contrast his pain and despair, a month later, in writing to Diane de Polignac in Russia, is clear from every line.

The Comte de Provence assumed the regency and named Artois 'Lieutenant-General of the Kingdom'. It was in this capacity that Artois made the hazardous winter journey to St Petersburg, arriving there in the middle of March. Catherine the Great, though by now advanced in years, was always glad to have a good-looking addition to her entourage. Artois was received with royal honours but the only practical result of the visit was a quantity of empty promises, a jewelled sword and some good advice. 'You are', she said to him, 'one of the great princes of Europe, but it is necessary sometimes to forget your station and to be a courageous partisan. Go to Brittany without waiting on negotiations. Take with you only a few men, but wise and prudent, enterprising and resolute.'

Artois adopted her ideas with apparent enthusiasm. In France there were still determined pockets of resistance to the Revolution and nowhere was that resistance so strong as in Brittany and in the Vendée. After what, in his own eyes, had been his triumph in Russia, Artois decided to visit England, and on 16 May, thanks to a frigate put at his disposal by Catherine the Great, he arrived at Hull. The outcome was humiliating. The Russian Ambassador, Worontzov, no doubt privily warned by Catherine, did not take Artois seriously, either as a man of affairs or as a military leader, since in his view Artois 'was governed by men without ideas and was incapable of commanding a battalion'. The British Government, equally, were embarrassed by Artois's arrival since it regarded the Comte de Provence as the only accredited representative of the French royal house. Fortunately there was to hand the excuse of Artois debts—by now estimated at two million I.O.Us. Artois was accordingly warned that under English law he ran the risk of imprisonment should he land. He had no alternative but to set sail and a month later we find him once again in Hamm, greeted by the ever open arms of Louise de Polastron.

Tragic intelligence soon reached them. First, the execution, in October, of Marie-Antoinette, followed, a month later, by the death of Yolande, Duchesse de Polignac, worn out by the privations of exile. Louise de Polastron's grandfather, the amiable Monsieur Rougeot, once so proud of his grand-daughter's social success, died by the guillotine in May 1794, as did Artois's aunt, Madame Elizabeth, the following day.

In the meantime Artois, although deeply distressed, fulminated and did nothing. It was as if he had never heard the counsel of Catherine the Great nor paid heed to the heroic if unavailing resistance in the west of France. 'He has so cradled himself with illusion, he has so cradled me,' said

Vaudreuil in a letter to the Comte d'Antraigues of 14 October 1793, 'that I have lost part of my confidence. Lyons, the Vendée, Toulon or the tomb—all that would become him. The rest is worthless.' This, from Artois's closest friend, is damaging evidence.

Suddenly, in August 1794, the situation changed. Artois received word that he should report to the Duke of York, who was commanding the British troops in Holland, at his headquarters in Rotterdam. The Duke would arrange for his passage to London. Once again there was an unexplained setback. Artois found himself no longer needed, and when the revolutionary army forced the evacuation of the Netherlands by the British he was left behind in Hamm. For once, however, Artois appears not to have accepted the situation with his usual ineffective apathy. After a grim winter about which little is known, but during which he and those around him were often short of food, he was at last allowed to embark near Bremerhaven on the British warship *Asia* and on 7 August 1795 arrived at Portsmouth.

At Portsmouth the news was bad. In the first place, a French and British expedition to the Quiberon Peninsula in Brittany had ended in calamity and the massacre of Frenchmen by Frenchmen. The second was the death of the wretched Louis XVII in the Temple, the cold of that grim building having eaten into his rickety bones. The Comte de Provence was now Louis XVIII and Artois, as his next eldest brother, was, by long tradition, entitled to the appellation 'Monsieur'.

With one of his rare bursts of energy Artois demanded the command of a second expedition. After much hesitation on the part of the British Government his request was granted. Under Artois's command a force of about four thousand men of mixed nationalities was to land on the coast of Brittany to give assistance to Charette, one of the chiefs of the *Chouans*, as the royalist insurgents were known. At the end of August a fleet of about sixty vessels set sail under the command of Admiral Sir John Warren.

A number of details essential to success were lacking. The expeditionary force had little idea where Charette's forces were to be found and where it could effectively make a landing on the French coast. There was no plan of campaign, no proper liaison with the royalists, and no military commander worthy of the name. Ill prepared as the expedition was, one thing must have been apparent even to Artois—the necessity of speedy action of some sort. This had been the tenor of every communication to him from Charette during the preceding year. To this necessity the fleet paid little heed and it was only after a leisurely voyage that, at the beginning of

October, Artois disembarked on the Ile d'Yeu, south of St Nazaire, some twenty miles from the French coast.

Meantime the situation on the mainland had deteriorated rapidly. Charette had, on 25 September 1795, at Saint-Cyr, near Nantes, sustained a major reverse and the remnants of his troops were being driven towards the shore. Reinforcement was vital. 'I beg of you', wrote Charette on 5 October, 'to select any point on the coast between Bourganeux and the Point of Aiguillon where you can bring on a named day some hundreds of mounted men and I shall be there without fail.'

On the Ile d'Yeu, equally, things were going from bad to worse. At first, while the good weather lasted, this charade of a military operation fared reasonably well. Artois himself was billeted in a small house in Port Joinville, in Artois's day known as Port Breton. On the other hand the local population had little sympathy for what they regarded as an invasion. The weather broke and the ill-clothed, ill-fed soldiers, a rag-bag of British, French and Germans, became sick with scurvy and shivered in makeshift camps. Some were reduced to burning the roof timbers of the church of Saint-Sauveur in order to keep warm, which did not endear them to the islanders. The French officers, faced with the hardships of a soldier's life, began to find it less than tolerable. A few gallant exceptions there were, but for the most part the *émigrés* were reluctant to move, complained loudly and expressed their desire to return to England. Artois and those around him were full of foreboding. Reports indicated a coastline almost wholly held by Republican troops. The sea was rough. Was it wise, was it, indeed, right to expose the person of a Royal Prince, an heir to the throne, to so many risks and dangers? Artois in the midst of this jeremaiad was incapable of making up his mind.

The story is told that Charette for his part was persuaded that Artois was about to land near the Ile de Ré. He gathered together what was left of his army and to this small kernel came nobles and peasants alike, encouraged by the prospect of meeting their Prince. Excitement grew and reached its pitch with the arrival of a vessel at Saint Jean-de-Mont. It was not Artois, only an aide-de-camp bringing another of Artois's eternal letters and a magnificent sword of honour. Charette was in despair. His reply to Artois was short. 'Tell the Prince,' he said, 'that he has signed my death warrant.' Whether or not this story is true does not matter. It symbolises the truth. Charette was captured, tried and shot at Nantes early the following year.

Artois's irresolution was brought to an end by the British Government. The expedition was recalled and the frigate *Jason* sent for the express purpose of bringing Artois to Britain. On 21 November 1795 *Jason* and the rest of the fleet raised anchor. For six weeks, the only six weeks in the twenty-five years between 1789 and 1814, Artois had found himself on French soil. He had achieved no personal advantage and to those he was sent to aid, his loyal *Chouans*, he had done irreparable harm by falsely raising their expectations.

Recriminations there were in plenty. The leaders of the resistance in the Vendée could not hide their disgust. One announced that he would henceforth enter the service of the Republic rather than remain under the orders of men who had abandoned him in so cowardly a fashion. Louis XVIII, who had set much store by the success of the expedition, was deeply disturbed and sarcasm throve throughout Europe. References to '*ce voyageur indéfatigable*', 'this indefatigable traveller,' mingled with the cries of distress. 'If I had been the Prince,' said Napoleon at a much later date, 'I would have crossed the sea in a nutshell.'

Excuses were, of course, equally abundant and each circumstance unfavourable to the landing was seized as a reason for not proceeding—the weather, the strength of the opposition, the perfidy of the English. It was also said that, if weakness there was, it was not the weakness of Artois but the pernicious influence of Louise de Polastron which had paralysed his fine character. This assertion was robustly demolished by the Duc d'Enghien—'If I had such a mistress, I would soon enough have landed her on the mainland of France.'

On his return to English waters Artois was confronted with difficulties of another kind. As has been said, large bills from his days at the head of the Army of the Princes remained unpaid. His creditors or their agents, armed with power of arrest, awaited him on the shore at Portsmouth. To avoid arrest Artois had no choice but to remain aboard *Jason* at anchor at Spithead where, with inexhaustible optimism, he sought in correspondence with his few surviving supporters in France to excuse himself by blaming the British Government.

The latter, in its turn, again found Artois a source of difficulty. The Government could have settled his debts but had it done so Artois would have been free to create further problems. With the end of the Terror in France the Government was considering a less bellicose attitude towards Paris. Artois may not have been a noteworthy success as a matador; his ability to wave a red cape was beyond question.

Accommodation for the Prince and his entourage could be found in the Palace of Holyroodhouse and this was the solution chosen by the British Government. No direct evidence of official thinking has been found, but the reasons are not difficult to understand. By the law of Scotland the Palace and its grounds provided an asylum for debtors from their creditors. The same law would thus effectively confine Artois within the bounds of the Sanctuary. Best of all, Edinburgh was four hundred miles from London.

The French historian, Jaques Vivent, has put it well, 'It was by putting him in prison that Artois was protected against the threat of imprisonment. In this one sees the sense of humour with which the English know how to colour their hypocrisy.'

On 22 December 1795 the Duke of Portland gave instructions to the Lord Provost of Edinburgh and to the Chief Baron of the Exchequer that Holyrood was to be put in readiness. The following day *Jason* set sail for Leith. Artois wrote to the Duc de Sérent, 'I leave for my sad exile . . . One would have to be a wizard to prophesy what will happen.'

CHAPTER 4

Early Days at the Palace of Holyrood

Artois's desire to have as little ceremony as possible on his arrival on 6 January has already been mentioned, but ceremony in fact followed. The gossip writer of the *Advertiser* reported two days later:

> Yesterday His Royal Highness the Comte d'Artois held his first levee at the Abbey at which the Lord President, the Lord Advocate, the Lord Provost and Magistrates and several Civil and Military Gentlemen attended and were presented to His Royal Highness. After the levee ended, His Royal Highness, accompanied by his suite, by Lord Adam Gordon, the Lord Advocate and Sir James Stirling, visited the suite of Royal apartments in the Palace, which we understand are ordered to be fitted up and furnished with all expedition for the reception of His Royal Highness and his son the Duke of Angouleme who is expected here soon from England.

According to another account, in the *Scots Magazine*, also present were Henry, third Duke of Buccleuch and his heir, Lord Dalkeith, a first meeting between the two families which in due course developed into close friendship and gave rise to many visits by Artois and his sons to Dalkeith Palace.

The Lord President of the Court of Session, mentioned by the *Advertiser*, was Ilay Campbell of Succoth. 'An able, ingenious, hard-working, commonplace man', says Omond, but that underestimates the man. He was the last Lord President to preside over the 'Auld Fifteen', the assembled bench of fifteen judges. They constituted an unruly mob and he managed them with considerable skill. Moreover, in a long retirement, he worked unstintingly for the many reforms to the Court of Session which had proved necessary.

The Lord Advocate was Robert Dundas of Arniston, born into the powerful Dundas clan, being a son of Lord President Dundas and a nephew of Henry Dundas, later Viscount Melville, at that date Secretary of State for War and the virtual ruler of Scotland. Omond considers that Robert Dundas 'was a man of very moderate talents, who would never have risen, save for the accident of his birth.' Cockburn, however, presents a more generous picture. 'He was a little, alert, handsome, gentleman-like man, with a countenance and air beaming with sprightliness and gaiety; and dignified by considerable fire, altogether inexpressibly pleasing.' He became a good friend to the French, entertained them at Arniston and when, in 1801, he became Chief Baron of Exchequer and in charge of Treasury disbursements in Scotland, an important figure in their lives. The third notable cited by the *Advertiser*, Sir James Stirling, had made a substantial fortune in the West Indies and in 1796 was a merchant and banker and the Lord Provost of Edinburgh.

A further levee was held three days later at which 'officers of the Royal Edinburgh Volunteers, in their uniforms, and several gentlemen of distinction paid their respects.' Indeed, it was reported in the daily papers that Artois was to hold a levee at Holyrood each Monday and Thursday and at first this appears to have been the case. Pryse Lockhart Gordon had been presented to Artois by Lord Adam Gordon and 'despite his slender acquaintance with French generally acted as a master of ceremonies.' His *Memoirs* provide the background to these early formalities. 'The judges and lawyers and all the respectable inhabitants of the metropolis attended the levées and brushed up their French.' It was General Drummond of Strathallan, who had been brought up in France during the exile of his father, who saved the day linguistically. The day needed saving.

> The mistakes which occurred at this modern court of Holyrood were sometimes not a little ludicrous. One gentleman on presenting an officer of a Highland regiment (now a lord) in his full costume said, 'voila, mon Prince, Monsieur G____, capitaine d'un regiment des Ecossais sauvage!'. The 'voila' and the 'sauvage' made his Royal Highness titter, and turning to General Drummond he asked for an explanation, who replied, 'the montagnard and sauvage were synonymous'. On another occasion, Lord ____ was desirous of telling the Duke that the adjutant-general kept a good table, and said, 'Monsieur le Général teint une bonne boutique!' which caused no small amusement.

Henry Mackenzie, the author of *The Man of Feeling* tells the same story and reveals that its subject was Lord Adam Gordon himself, of whom he says that Lord Adam organised the receptions and adds that, 'His Lordship wanted only one qualification for the office, not being a very good Frenchman and speaking French very imperfectly.'

Pryse Lockhart Gordon was also astonished at the gastronomic powers of the French.

There was also a weekly dinner at which I assisted ex officio. Until I had seen these Frenchmen, I thought the power of man was limited; one day a salmon three feet long, and not less than 25 lbs was put down as the second course and in a trice it disappeared. These festivities were, however, of short duration. It was discovered that feeding so many hungry wolves, and the expense of the establishment far exceeded Monsieur's means, and at the end of three or four months both the levées and the dinners were discontinued, much to his Royal Highness's satisfaction; who was now left to repose, and the society of his friends and 'followers'.

The Comte d'Artois's means were indeed limited. He had an allowance of £500 per month from the British Government and Angoulême had £300. These sums were not ungenerous taken in isolation but did not go far to satisfy the demands of a ravenous horde.

Artois himself made a favourable impression on Pryse Lockhart Gordon. 'I had frequent opportunities of conversing with him; his manners were extremely affable, at the same time dignified.'

Artois at this time can be seen in one of Kay's Edinburgh Portraits, walking arm in arm with Lord Adam Gordon. Artois's youthful looks remain, despite his fortieth year, but there is a trace of double chin and his waistline is distinctly more ample than that of his companion. Artois wears a simple civilian coat and light coloured breeches but, as if it were unthinkable that he should appear in public without such embellishments, his hat is trimmed with the white cockade and on his left chest he displays the large eight-pointed star of the Saint Esprit.

Around Artois quickly gathered the principal members of the group which had tied its future to his since the days of Versailles and Bagatelle. The first to arrive after the Comte d'Artois was his son, the Duc d'Angoulême, who reached Edinburgh on 21 January. His quarters not being in proper repair, said the press, he was accommodated in the apartments of Lord Breadalbane. Angoulême announced that he would 'see company for the present in the apartments of "Monsieur" on Mondays and Thursdays at noon', but there is no record that such receptions ever took place and it has been suggested that part of the difficulty lay in the high cost of wax candles. Normally the royal household made do with tallow.

Both father and son must have been moved by the news, which reached Edinburgh in early January, that Louis XVI's daughter, Madame Royale, '*l'orpheline du Temple*', had at last been released from her captivity in Paris and exchanged for certain hostages whom the Emperor in Vienna was holding against that event. There was little charity behind the move. The Emperor Francis had in mind the marriage of Madame Royale to his brother. If it could be maintained that the Salic Law had been abolished in France Madame Royale would then have a claim to the French crown in her own right and a dynastic alliance with France was very much in the interests of Austria. Thus for a spell she was to find that she had bartered a Parisian cell for a gilded cage in the Hofburg. The Edinburgh press followed her travels from France to Austria. As recorded in the *Advertiser* of 12 January:

> The Courrier Francais mentions her arrival at Chaumont. The axle tree of her carriage taking fire, for want of grease, she was compelled to walk the greater part of one stage. She was surrounded by an innumerable crowd on her arrival who were struck with awe and sympathy by her beauty and misfortunes. Her carriage being repaired she pursued her way, being treated throughout with the utmost respect.

Another early arrival, although she had been preceded by her parents, was Madame de Gontaut, together with her husband, the Marquis de Gontaut-Biron. Madame de Gontaut's father had been a tutor to Artois and after the Restoration of 1814, Madame de Gontaut played a similar role, becoming governess to the children of the Duc de Berry. She was one of the few present at Holyrood in 1796 to share with Artois the second Edinburgh exile of 1830. Madame de Gontaut, together with her two daughters and a lady's maid, and with her husband at the reins, had travelled from London to Edinburgh in a one-horse phaeton, taking fifteen days for the journey. A phaeton, being designed only for four, including the driver, and having no cover, the pilgrimage must have been singularly uncomfortable. Madame de Gontaut has left us her *Mémoires* which are a valuable source for both periods of exile, although they lack both objectivity and accuracy. The *Mémoires* were not written until 1853, when Madame de Gontaut was aged 80, and for her Artois never ceased to be the object of a veneration which she never troubled to conceal.

Whatever defects her account may have as historical narrative, here is how Madame de Gontaut recalled the scene more than half a century later:

> I have to admit that our arrival at Edinburgh struck my heart with sadness: Holyroodhouse is situated in the middle of the old town in the poorest and most unhealthy quarter. The chateau has a sad and grim appearance. It is protected like a fortress and appeared to me like a prison.

'Monsieur', she continued,

> was waiting in the courtyard for our equipage to arrive: he came towards us with his accustomed grace, at once so frank and noble, and seemed to be grateful for the journey that we had undertaken for his sake. In the face of this calm and noble fortitude I tried to kneel but I was told, 'Your mother awaits you. I am not in my own home; I cannot have any friends to stay with me here but I ask that they settle not far from me; your lodging is over there in the square where we have a small French colony and, God willing, the days will pass.' He said that my husband should come to dine with him whenever he wished but, having only a modest establishment, he could only ask the ladies for tea.

From Madame de Gontaut we learn that although on his arrival Artois was accompanied only by 'M.le Comte Francois Descars' and the 'Chevalier de Puysegur', nevertheless as soon as they learnt of Monsieur's plight 'his faithful followers arrived from Russia, from Germany and from London'. The Comte Descars or, more usually, d'Escars, became an envoy to Sweden and Prussia during the emigration and after the Restoration of the monarchy in 1814, *Premier Maître d'Hôtel*, the equivalent of the Lord Chamberlain.

The roll-call of those who were to base themselves in Edinburgh for the next three years—in some cases much longer—or who were to be constant visitors, reads like the list of guests at a private supper party at the Petit Trianon. Indeed, of those recorded as having been invited to dine privately with Marie-Antoinette one evening in June 1780, all save the Queen had foregathered in Edinburgh by March 1797. Louise de Polastron was there, of course; also her devoted school friends from the Abbaye de Panthémont, Mesdames de Lage and de Poulpry and Agläe de Polignac, Duchesse de Guiche, whose mother, Yolande de Polastron, Duchesse de Polignac, had been so instrumental in bringing Artois and Louise de Polastron together. When necessary all four seem to have crowded into Louise's little house.

As regards Louise herself, she was only 32 when she arrived in Edinburgh in the early weeks of 1796, but she was already showing the early signs of consumption. In October of that year Artois writes to Vaudreuil, 'I am tormented by the health of our friend; she has had a fever of the nerves and has suffered much and it is only today that she feels better.' 'Publicly established as part of [Artois's] household, this liaison was so well known that it had ceased to be a scandal', wrote Madame de Boigne. This was not wholly true of Edinburgh society, as will be seen from a report by Napoleon's spy some years later.

For a time at least, the French contingent at Holyrood included Agläe's two brothers, Armand de Polignac and his brother Jules, later Prince de Polignac and later still the ill-advised and ill-advising first minister of the Comte d'Artois when, in 1824, he ascended the throne as Charles X. Absent was their mother, the Duchesse de Polignac, who had died in 1793. History records that her husband bore this loss with '*assez de philosophie*,' but that her lover, Artois's inseparable companion, the Comte de Vaudreuil, was inconsolable. Inconsolable, that is, for two years. In 1795, at the age of fifty, he had married his cousin Josephine, then aged twenty. They too were frequent visitors to Holyrood. From the many letters exchanged between Artois and Vaudreuil during the emigration the latter emerges as as a loyal and not unintelligent man who in another context might have achieved much more.

Vaudreuil's father came from an old Languedoc family with an established tradition of overseas service—his grandfather had been Governor-General of Canada—and his mother was the daughter of a rich sugar planter in San Domingo. Vaudreuil was thus possessed of the essential combination of lineage and wealth to ensure his welcome at Versailles. There he soon found his true métier as master of ceremonies to the Polignac clan. Vaudreuil was a person of great charm and manner, a noted raconteur, and something of a wit. It has been said of him that he assiduously put into effect the advice of an old courtier: 'Speak well of everyone, while always waiting for the moment to apply the second imperative—ask for anything that may be a-going.' His portrait by Drouais, which hangs in Trafalgar Square, shows him elegantly dressed, his armour nonchalantly discarded at his feet, pointing with proprietorial pride to the map of San Domingo.

Nonetheless one of his contemporaries saw him in a different light. The Comtesse de Boigne had known him both at Versailles and during the emigration in London:

> I saw a great deal of the Comte de Vaudreuil but could never discover for what reason his contemporaries regarded him so highly. He had been a leader of that school of exaggeration which prevailed before the Revolution, enthusiastic for trivialities and careless of important matters. With the help of money which he drew from the royal treasury, he had become the patron of various minor Virgils who praised him in couplets. At the house of Madame Lebrun he would

> strike an attitude before a picture and patronise artists. He lived with them on familiar terms and kept his fine manners for the drawing-room of Madame de Polignac but in private revealed his ingratitude towards the Queen of whom I have heard him speak in the most disparaging terms. In exile and old, his claims became ridiculous, and he was forced to see his wife's lovers pay the household bills by presents which she pretended to have won in a lottery.

Like those of Madame de Gontaut, the Memoirs of the Comtesse de Boigne are the product of old age. Unlike the Duchesse de Gontaut, however, who thought ill of no-one, Madame de Boigne is invariably catty and critical, and thus, of the two, her memoirs are the more enjoyable. Madame de Gontaut describes the Comtesse de Vaudreuil as 'pious as an angel' and the truth matters little. The magnetism of Vaudreuil and his young wife did much to ease the longueurs of Holyrood for the sad circle of *émigrés*.

At or near Holyrood, in addition to those members of the Polignac family who have already been mentioned, also in Edinburgh were the widower Duc de Polignac and his sister Diane. She had at one time been attached to the household of the Comtesse d'Artois but had shown no disposition to share her mistress's self-imposed banishment from Versailles. As the honorary head of a noble chapter of nuns in Lorraine, Diane de Polignac bore the title of Comtesse in her own right. In many ways she was the most talented and unusual member of the family. Despite her singular ugliness she achieved an unexpected ascendancy over Marie-Antoinette and was responsible for the favours, financial and otherwise, shown to her beautiful sister-in-law. It is a tribute to the personality of Diane de Polignac that she not only achieved a son, by the Marquis d'Autichamp, but as her '*jeune ami*' had him reside with her at Versailles. 'As avaricious as she was immoral', comments the Comtesse de Boigne with an audible sniff.

Given that Artois was influenced throughout his life by one or more members of the Polignac family, in which we may, by marriage at least, include Louise de Polastron, it is appropriate to say something of its origins.

The family name is said to derive from Apollo, and if that pedigree cannot be traced with certainty there is no doubt that a Hercule de Polignac was one of the earliest to answer the call of Peter the Hermit to join in the First Crusade at the end of the eleventh century. From this era dates the original castle which bears the family name and which dominates the northern approaches to Le Puy. In more recent times Melchior de Polignac was the ambassador sent, in 1713, by Louis XIV to the Netherlands to negotiate the Treaty of Utrecht. It says much for his skill that he managed to achieve a surprisingly good peace for France after her reverses at the hands of Marlborough and Prince Eugène of Savoy. In the same year he became Cardinal, and, symbolically enough for this story, there exist two magnificent Roman paintings by Pannini, once the property of the Duke of Leeds, the one showing the ceremonial visit of Cardinal de Polignac to St Peter's, the other the visit to S. Paolo Fuori le Mura of Cardinal York, the younger brother of Prince Charles Edward Stuart. Just over half a century later the grand-nephew of one was to take refuge in the ancestral home of the other and the role of exile was reversed.

The Paris Archives contain a list of Artois's household as it eventually established itself. It is noteworthy for magnificent titles borne by some, titles which were without substance. It is worth giving the list in full: Chastenay-Puységur and d'Escars shared the duties of Captain of the Guard; Etienne de Damas, Duverne and Lallemant were equerries; Charles de Rivière the first aide-de-camp; Monseigneur de Conzié, the Duc de Sérent and the Baron de Roll, Members of Council; Belleville, Treasurer. Forestier was the Doctor and Duverne the Valet de Chambre. Some of these have already been mentioned; others will emerge in the narrative.

It would be wrong, however, to think of the French colony in Edinburgh as static. A nucleus apart, there was much coming and going between Edinburgh and London and, by the devious and dangerous routes which remained open, between Edinburgh and the partisans in the west of France or with Louis XVIII's court wherever it had found shelter.

Levees and dinners apart, the initial stir in Edinburgh appears to have been considerable. If Monsieur could travel beyond the Abbey bounds only on a Sunday, his family and friends were not so restricted and they made use of the one carriage which he maintained.

The Duc d'Angoulëme was a target for the go-ahead entrepreneur. The following advertisement in the *Edinburgh Advertiser* of 4 March 1796 merits quotation:

BY DESIRE OF HIS ROYAL HIGHNESS
THE DUKE D'ANGOULEME
for the Benefit of M. Bologna and family.
On Monday first, the 7th of March will be exhibited at
ROYAL CIRCUS

A variety of pleasing amusements
In particular: for the first time in EUROPE will be exhibited
A GRAND BALLOON
Fixed in the Centre of the Stage, Turning Horizontally at the same time,
Surrounded with Fire-Works, in the
Display of which, the BALLOON will separate into Four Quarters,
exhibiting a
TRANSPARENCY OF GOD SAVE THE KING
In Brilliant Fire
When a Great Variety of New DANCING, SINGING and TIGHT-ROPE DANCING,
and various feats of Equestrian Exercise, Pantomime etc
will be Performed
A GRAND FIRE-WORK
For the First time, a Match between
TWO FIERY DRAGONS
Which will run three times from the Stage to the Gallery; a piece of
Fire-Work never before attempted

The 'Royal Circus' was situated at the head of Leith Walk at its junction with Broughton Street and for a time contested the right to the name 'Theatre Royal'. At one time Signor Bologna seems to have been owner but in 1796 it was owned by one Jones, Signor Bologna vanishing from the scene shortly afterwards.

On a number of other occasions the Duc d'Angoulême attended performances at the Theatre Royal, usually accompanied by the Duchess of Buccleuch. The *Scots Magazine*, for example, reports that he and his suite attended the theatre on 14 March and

> were most cordially received by a very crowded and fashionable audience. The decorations of the box fitted up for His Royal Highness did credit to the taste and liberality of the Manager, the festoons were a dark purple satin, edged with a deep silver fringe and lined with white muslin. His Majesty's Arms, elegantly finished, were placed at top.

As the Theatre Royal, then on the North Bridge, was in financial straits, it may be assumed that the liberality of the manager was not entirely selfless.

Angoulême was also initiated into another activity. Again Pryse Lockhart Gordon tells the story:

> I had the honour to attend the Duke d'Angoulême when he made his first essay as a fox-hunter. Mr. Baird of Newbyth furnished His Royal Highness with a horse; the Caledonian Hounds were at Haddington and we went in a

post-chaise to meet them. The weather was favourable, the scent high and a fox was soon found. I recommended the young Prince to follow Mr. Baird as closely as he could, as he was acquainted with the country. He did so, and as all the gates had previously been opened and the fox ran gallantly, there was a sharp run for ten minutes when the hounds came to a fault.

Diplomacy, it seems, had been at work.

Laurie had stolen away, or given them the slip, but I afterwards learned that an earth which the huntsman thought reynard would try, had been left open on purpose, for the country beyond was enclosed, and Mr. Baird, who had the direction of the day's sport, did not wish that a descendant of Henry the Fourth should run the risk of breaking his neck. If this was true nothing could have been better managed. The youth had a gallop of four miles, and was delighted with the sport. As he was engaged to dine with the Earl of Haddington, I took my leave, and returned to Edinburgh in the chaise. At the next levee Monsieur thanked me for my attention to his son, who, he said, could now talk of nothing but the *grande chasse au reynard*!

On 30 June 1796 Holyrood was the scene of the election of sixteen Scottish peers to sit in the House of Lords. This appears to have been a social occasion of some importance as the *Caledonian Mercury* reports the attendance of 'a great number of ladies of rank and fashion'. Artois was there and many of his courtiers. Afterwards the peers who had been returned gave a party at Fortune's new Tontine Tavern in Princes Street. Many of Artois's group were there, together with the military and legal establishment of Edinburgh.

Madame de Gontaut states that the Scottish nobility were pressing in their invitations. She herself was well supplied with introductions. Apart from the Buccleuchs there was their daughter-in-law, Harriet, Countess of Dalkeith. At Pinkie there was Lady Hope, née Wedderburn, whose father at the age of sixteen had followed Prince Charles Edward Stuart and whose grandfather had been executed as a Jacobite. At Inveresk House Madame de Gontaut met Lady Hope's sister-in-law, Lady Wedderburn, and her sister, Lady Hampden. Of these encounters Madame de Gontaut wrote in 1853: 'The tender affection of the two elder followed me to their grave, and the youngest, Lady Hope, is kind enough to keep warm her friendship towards me'.

'Monsieur', himself, the Comte d'Artois, on his Sunday excursions, again according to Madame de Gontaut, 'went out morning and evening. He was invited everywhere and everyone hastened to welcome him. A visit paid by him, to these good and excellent Scots, was an honour and a celebration'. This statement must, however, be seen in perspective. The early levées apart, there was little official entertaining by Artois. In the first place his resources were too limited and in the second place, as we shall see from one of Vaudreuil's letters, Artois felt that given the misfortunes of his country and of those who had suffered in the Royalist interest, all ostentation was to be avoided.

Edinburgh in its turn was sympathetic. Sir Walter Scott echoed the feelings of many when he wrote to Lady Louisa Stuart, the youngest daughter of the former prime minister, the Earl of Bute:

> You remember the lines of Chapelain (Chastelain or Molinet) [Chastelain and Molinet were Renaissance chroniclers of Burgundy, evidence of Scott's astonishing range of reading] on the succour he received in Scotland, 'ever kind to banished princes though so rude a country.' I forget the French words, but that I think is the meaning, which recurred strongly to my mind when I saw 'Monsieur' come to our old Abbey.

The Duc d'Angoulême, exceptionally for a Bourbon, occupied himself with military affairs. On the Continent, events continued to favour the French Republic, and the fear of invasion, which was to last for the next decade, was beginning to make itself apparent even in Scotland. Volunteer and Yeomanry regiments were everywhere being formed.

The first regiment of Edinburgh Volunteers, according to Francis Steuart,

> were called 'The True Blues' and their uniform was blue with red flashings. The Duc d'Angoulême was a constant attender at their drills, but 'Monsieur' could never conquer his repugnance to their uniform, which reminded him too strongly of that of the National Guard from which his brother had suffered so many things, and once, when an officer came to one of his levées at Holyrood in this terrible uniform, he was seriously disconcerted.

It was while Angoulême was engaged in this activity that he became the subject of Kay's engraving which was given the title 'The Great and the Small are there'. It shows the slight figure of the Duc d'Angoulême looking as if his boots were too tight and very self-conscious beside the huge person of Major-General Roger Ayton of Inchdairney and who, by contrast, appears relaxed and jovial. Whether with malice or not, the artist has positioned Angoulême some distance to the rear of the troops.

All in all, as shown by Sir Walter Scott's letter, public reaction to the

French *émigrés* was sympathetic, a sympathy encapsulated by a monstrous piece of doggerel which appeared in the *Scots Chronicle* for 2 March 1796:

> O Scotia! take me to thy arms.
> Thy friendly arms o stretch to me!
> My native land has lost her charms,
> From Gallia's shore I come to thee.
> Oh! let the voice of woe prevail.
> Thy tenderness will sooth my grief.

So much then for the public face of the French colony in the opening months of 1796. The private face, the fears and hopes, the quarrels and some of the many comings and goings are kept for a later chapter. Something, too, will be said of Artois's place in the wider European scene. Prisoner, as he was, in Holyrood, he still remained Lieutenant-General of the French Kingdom and nominally, at least, responsible for royalist operations in the west of Europe. Many were the schemes discussed within the walls of the palace between Artois and his immediate circle and the emissaries who came and went from London or who made the hazardous journey via the Channel Islands from occupied Brittany or the Vendée.

CHAPTER 5

Quality of Life at Holyroodhouse

On his first arrival at Holyrood Artois was conducted to the apartments of Lord Adam Gordon. These were in the south-west part of the palace and were intended only as a temporary refuge.

Of the original Palace of Holyroodhouse there remains today only one rectangular tower, some four stories high, with turrets or 'engaged rounds' at each corner. This was part of the palace built for James IV between the years 1498 and 1501 at the time when the capital of Scotland was moving from Stirling to Edinburgh. The second and major part of the Palace is an essay in the Palladian manner designed by Sir William Bruce of Balkcaskie in the years following 1671. This incorporates the James IV tower in its north-west corner and follows three sides of an arcaded court, completed by a companion tower at the south-west. The west side of the courtyard is formed by a two-storey screen containing the main entrance and surmounted by a clock turret and a passage at the level of the first floor, incorporating the present Household dining room, which links the James IV tower and the William Bruce version. Sir John Summerson has said that there is no subtlety in the design but the result is not inelegant, and despite its limited scale the courtyard façade of the eastern wing blends severity with dignity and calls to mind Bruce's other major achievement, Kinross House.

At worst the present building is a far cry from the ruined medieval chateau with 'all the apparatus of the Middle Ages which Walter Scott so well brought to life', to quote the French historian, Lucas-Dubreton, writing in the 1920s. In the company of other modern French historians it is plain that he was unable to differentiate between the Palace of Holyroodhouse and Edinburgh Castle. It is only in one of the most recent biographies of Artois, that by André Castelot, that the author admits past errors and gives Holyrood its rightful place. The culprit is, of course, Victor Hugo whose lugubrious poem begins:

Holyrood! Holyrood! la ronce est sur tes dalles.
Le chevreau broute au bas de tes tours féodales.

The couplet loses much in translation: 'Holyrood! Holyrood! The bramble bush grows on your paving stones. The young goat grazes beneath your feudal towers'. Hugo did not write his poem, *Les Rayons et les Ombres*, until 1839, and—so far as is known—without ever having visited the scene which he describes with so much romantic agony. Nevertheless it explains why, as late as 1967, so restrained a writer as Jean-Paul Garnier cannot resist the phrase 'an abandoned feudal fortress lost in the mists of Scotland'. Perhaps it was inevitable. If the theme is the contrast with the imperial glory of Versailles it is difficult to resist the image of dilapidation and this in its turn induces the coloured epigram such as, to quote the nineteenth century writer Nettement: 'Holyrood, weeping for its kings, made a fitting home for the Bourbons weeping for their motherland.'

It must, none the less, be admitted that in 1796 the Palace of Holyroodhouse had certain major disadvantages as a royal residence. Arnot, in his History of Edinburgh, published in 1788, after explaining that, 'The only apartments which are worth viewing are those possessed by the Duke of Hamilton, heritable keeper of the Palace. These occupy all that remains of the old palace,' goes on to say:

> These chambers which are called the royal apartments occupy three sides of the square on the first floor. On the north is a spacious gallery, of which, however, the height bears no proportion to the length. This apartment is entirely hung with pictures of a race of a hundred and eleven monarchs, through an imaginary series of upwards of two thousand years.

There, of course, they still remain, a unique decorative feature.

Arnot thought otherwise:

> The folly of the legend, and the baseness of the execution, in portraying these monarchs, whether real or imaginary, would make it for the honour of the country that they were utterly destroyed. We saw, indeed, that an attempt had been made at their destruction which was not easily to be accounted for. Not only were most of them hacked and slashed, but in many of them large pieces were cut out.

This

> was owing to General Hawley's having thought proper after the defeat of the King's army at Falkirk, to quarter his troops in the gallery of this palace, and these *well disciplined troops* thought that they could not better manifest their loyalty to King George than by defacing and hewing in pieces every representation of the Scottish monarchs.

Arnot continues:

> We afterwards went through a suit of rooms, one of which has been intended for a state bed-chamber, and the two next for a drawing-room and dining-room . . . In this suit the rooms are wainscotted with oak; the festoons of flowers and foliage over the doors and mantle pieces are well executed; but the stucco ornaments of the roofs, similar to all of that period are heavy.

Of the apartments on the 'south' side Arnot says that they have

> never been finished but in a very pityful manner. We found them made use of as lumber rooms for some of the nobility who have lodgings in the palace.

One of these was known as Lord Dunmore's lodgings, in fact on the north side under the long gallery, of which 'the apartments are few, of a pityful size, miserably furnished and no furniture in them with the exception of the large Van Dyke painting of Charles I and Henrietta-Maria.' Arnot sums up his impression by saying, 'This magnificent palace is no use whatever except the part which is occupied by the Duke of Hamilton; and the whole is falling into decay for want of being possessed, and kept in repair.'

Some improvement took place when Lord Adam Gordon was given permission to live in the Palace and the sum of £1400 expended by him and his wife on repairs was refunded by the Treasury in 1794. Lord Adam's quarters were, however, those granted to the Duke of Hamilton in the older part of the palace and the repairs would not seem to have benefited the remainder.

Substantial work, however, was carried out consequent upon Artois's arrival in 1796 and during the following decade. A Treasury Report of 1807 summarises the matter:

> In consequence of the very complete repair which the palace underwent in the year 1795 (sic), it is now in a more complete and better state than it has been at any period since the Union, except with regard to the leaden roof, which we are informed is in several parts very much washed and decayed.

The whole affair was, needless to say, approached by the Treasury with due caution. The original instructions for the reception of Artois and his retinue were issued from Whitehall by the Duke of Portland on 22 December 1795 to, among others, the Lord Provost of Edinburgh and the Lord Chief Baron of the Exchequer:

> You will of course limit your views to the object which is solely the accommodation of the persons I have mentioned in such a manner as will best suit their convenience and be least productive of expense.

The Duke of Portland specially directed that Artois and the Duc d'Angoulême should be lodged in Holyrood together with the necessary servants who, he supposed, would number six. Monsieur's retinue—some seven gentlemen, one secretary, two chaplains and one physician, 'may be lodged anywhere within or out of the Palace in such a manner as may be least likely to give umbrage or offence.'

Work appears to have been begun with commendable speed. On 24 January 1796 Lord Adam Gordon is writing to the Duke of Portland as follows, 'I have the honour to report to your Grace that the repairs in the King's apartment are going better on—that the water-closets are ordered.'

The furniture apart, detailed accounts no longer exist. The originals were probably destroyed in the fire which took place in the Exchequer Office in Parliament Square on 11 November 1811, but an overall picture can be obtained from a surviving account covering the years 1796 to 1801. Under the heading 'Expenses on account of Monsieur's suit upon his arrival at Holyroodhouse before his establishment was formed,' we find such items as 'John Bayle, Vintner—for Provisions and Necessaries furnished—£124.19.8½', (the '½' pence reveals a steady bureaucratic hand) or 'Messrs. Bell and Rannie for Wine -£61.' These entries perhaps explain Pryse Lockhart Gordon's comments on the gourmandising powers of the French nobility.

A substantial item, £974, was the expense of 'additional lodgings', the 'Royal apartments not being sufficient for the accommodation of Monsieur's suit.' The sum included the construction of a temporary office for the Adjutant-General, as a consequence of Artois's taking over Lord Adam Gordon's lodging.

Once Monsieur was in residence a building programme was put in hand. 'Major Work', which included the construction of a porter's lodge, came to more than £2,000. In addition, over the five-year period of the accounts, the total for plastering, painting, carpentry, glazing and plumbing exceeded £1,500. To put this expenditure in perspective, at this time a substantial country house with stabling could be built for £3,000.

Furnishing was on an equally generous scale. During the same period the payments to 'Messrs. Young, Trotter Hamilton upholsterers in Edinb. for Furniture of Various kinds Bed and Table Linen China Glassware and

Others' was £2,734.2.3 as well as £146 to 'Mr. Dironi' for mirrors and £78 to 'William Couper, Upholsterer, for Carpets'.

Young, Trotter and Hamilton's accounts are preserved among the Laing manuscripts in Edinburgh University Library. How that magpie, David Laing, came by them will never be known, but they have been meticulously studied by Margaret Swain and many items of furniture now in the palace have been identified as having been made for the Comte d'Artois.

Margaret Swain has put it succinctly:

> The furnishings supplied were by no means regal. They were similar in all respects to those bought for gentlemen's residences in Edinburgh's New Town and the many country mansions that were being built and refurnished all over Scotland. The furniture was mahogany, well made, refined and unostentatious. Except for the twenty dining room chairs, covered in satin hair cloth, most of the upholstered chairs were finished in unbleached linen, with slip covers of printed cotton chintz to match window curtains and belongings.

In short, the sort of furniture with which, two centuries later, it is a pleasure to live rather than to view from behind the looped cords of the greatest houses.

It is probable that what Messrs. Young, Trotter and Hamilton provided had little to do with Artois's personal taste. It is more likely that it represents what the Treasury and, in particular their man on the spot, Patrick Murray, the King and Lord Treasurer's Remembrancer, was prepared to sanction and what Young, Trotter and Hamilton had in stock or could quickly provide from their pattern books. Certainly the contrast with what had been supplied to Artois in France is striking. The fantastic chairs *à la turque* for the Paris house have been mentioned. Another example of known Artois provenance is the pair of tulipwood encoignures, now in the Wallace Collection, designed by Joubert in 1773 for Artois's apartments at Versailles. They reflect the new classical vogue, but their severity is broken by gilt-bronze mounts—swags, acanthus leaves, gladitorial masks and trophies of exuberant vitality. Margaret Swain also instances the cylinder-top desk of kingwood and tulipwood, veneered with Artois's arms, which is now in Buckingham Palace. Once again, one asks, Artois's taste or the fashion of the moment? More probably the latter. For example, Joubert was successively *ébéniste ordinaire du Garde-Meuble de la Couronne* and *ébéniste du Roi* and to him commissions would automatically go. Indeed, the entire roll-call of the great Parisian craftsmen were at Artois's command; Oeben, Reisener and Jacob among the cabinet-makers, Gouthière and Thômire for the *bronze doré*, Lepaute for clocks, and there is little to suggest that Artois concerned himself greatly with such matters even at Versailles or in Paris. By 1796 it is probable that the hardships of his travels had taught him that a warm fire, security and peace to play whist with Louise were all that was needed. The walls of Holyrood and the cabinet-makers of Edinburgh provided him with much more than that.

One puzzle remains. There is, in the collection of the Duke of Buccleuch, a classical seascape rather in the manner of Vernet or Lacroix de Marseilles. It entered the Buccleuch collection by purchase in 1830 from the grandson of Lady Elizabeth Murray, daughter of the first Earl of Dunmore, to whom it had been given by Artois. It hung in Artois's dining-room at Holyrood and is inscribed '*Elizabeth pour son frère D'Artois 1792*'. How did Artois receive the painting? In 1792 Madame Elizabeth, who died by the guillotine in 1794, was virtually a prisoner in the Tuileries and Artois was at Coblenz or, at the end of the year, in flight after the disasters of Valmy and Jemappes. The painting is traditionally ascribed to Madame Elizabeth herself. Can this be so? It would seem far too professional a work to be by her hand.

Instructions had been given by the Duke of Portland to provide stabling at or near the palace for six horses, and this was duly done. 'With regard to the stable and coach house, (we understand the only offices of the kind in the palace) they were fitted up and completely repaired by our order at a very considerable expense—and an addition built to them for the accommodation of Monsieur and his son the Duke de Berry', the Lord Commissioners of His Majesty's Treasury were told.

As is so often the case with accounts it is the miscellaneous items which provide the third dimension. To revert to the synopsis for the years 1796 to 1801. James Gordon received £121 for constructing the water-closets. Dicksons provided shrubs for the 'back area'; the 'Palace Clock' was repaired and there was a payment to 'John Medina Limner' for furnishing three paintings and 'Repairing Portraits in Gallery'. This John Medina, who was principally a copyist, was a grandson of the better-known and much more accomplished John Baptiste de Medina. One might have supposed that candles were the principal source of illumination but there are also payments to Robert Brown for 'Patent Lamps' and to William Darling, 'Oilman' for lighting lamps in the palace.

Not all Edinburgh tradesmen were impeccable. On 8 February 1796,

James Baird, Clerk to the Exchequer, is writing in fury to Messrs. Cameron and Watson, painters:

> Your paper in my opinion is no Estimate—you have made it so general that it is impossible to understand it—no price per yard is mentioned, no rooms taken notice of—you reserve to yourselves the liberty of painting the whole palace—whereas the Barons [of Exchequer] neither wish nor want more done than the Royal Apartments. Their Lordships instructions go no further—and if you without proper or legal authority paint any other part of the Palace but the Royal Apartments, Take leave to acquaint you that you will not receive your pay from this office, as you never received any order for executing more work than the said Royal Apartments.

Young, Trotter and Hamilton's account and other sources enable one to identify the principal rooms occupied by Artois and his suite, essentially those on the first floor of the east wing. Artois's sitting room adjoined the long gallery. Next to it, to the south, were the powdering closet and then the state bedroom. This was followed by the private drawing room. Opposite, facing the courtyard, were rooms for servants and for the secretary, Monsieur Belleville and the Comte d'Escars. The first-floor rooms in the south wing formed part of Lord Adam Gordon's suite. These were, in turn, the levee room, which is the large room now known as the morning drawing room, followed by the dining room, now the evening drawing room. Next came a billiard room, now the throne room, equipped, the accounts tell us, with, 'A Billiard table 12 feet by 6 feet of mahogany strongly framed and finished in the best manner covered with fine double milled green Cloth with a complete Sett of balls, queues, Maces etc.' at a price of £40. In the south-west tower there was a further drawing room, in what had been the meeting place of the old Scottish Privy Council, and, in the entrance screen, the modern household dining room, was Lord Adam Gordon's library. The east end of the long gallery served as a chapel and Presbyterian scruple accepted the supply of suitable furnishing. One of the two mahogany 'kneeling chairs' has survived and has been identified by Margaret Swain.

The upper floors of the palace are a warren of smaller rooms, and it was here that the Duc d'Angoulême and many of the suite and servants were housed. More than the royal apartments, however, were to be required. In March 1796 Lord Adam Gordon's lodging was formally taken over for the French and Dr Moore, the Underkeeper of the palace, was notified to that effect by the Barons of Exchequer. This was later to cause confusion and an irate exchange of letters from Lord Breadalbane and his man of business. Lord Breadalbane had received, in 1781, a grant of lodgings on the second floor of the south wing, and had temporarily lent some of his rooms 'to oblige Lord Adam Gordon under an obligation to restore'. These evidently were taken over with the rest of Lord Adam's lodging and it was a long time before they were returned to Lord Breadalbane. The Underkeeper of the palace, Dr John Moore, embroiled in these negotiations, deserves a passing mention. He had been tutor and physician to the eighth Duke of Hamilton on his grand tour to Switzerland and Italy in the 1770s and had been rewarded not only by an annuity but by the office of Underkeeper, the Dukes of Hamilton being the Hereditary Keepers of the palace. He was the author of a novel, *Zeluco*, which influenced Byron's *Childe Harold*, and he was the father of General Sir John Moore of Corunna fame.

Accordingly, one way and another, 'Monsieur' found himself not unworthily quartered. If Holyroodhouse was not Versailles it was greatly to be preferred to his most recent dwelling in Port Breton on the Ile d'Yeu and a world away from the privations of Hamm.

CHAPTER 6

Debtors and Sanctuary

More immediately important to Monsieur than the comfort of his quarters was the knowledge that within the walls surrounding the abbey sanctuary or Girth, to use the old Scots word, he was safe from imprisonment at the hands of his creditors.

The sanctuary constituted by the Palace of Holyroodhouse and the surrounding area embraced Arthur's seat and the present-day Queen's Park. The full significance of this right of sanctuary belongs to one of the obscurer by-ways of legal history but a word of explanation is necessary in order to appreciate the reasons for Artois's virtual incarceration for a period of more than two years.

Until the passing of the Debtors (Scotland) Act of 1880 imprisonment for debt was the regular sanction against the debtor who could not or would not pay. How this came about in the first place is a complex story involving a conflict between the medieval civil courts, which were reluctant to see a debtor prevented by imprisonment from fulfilling his feudal obligations of service, and the church courts, always anxious to increase their jurisdiction, which were happy to offer the compulsitor of prison, the *squalor carceris*, to the creditor seeking a remedy. By the seventeenth century at the latest the civil courts in Scotland had absorbed the competences of the pre-Reformation ecclesiastical courts and had developed a system of enforcing their judgements against debtors, full of ritual, known as Letters of Horning and Caption. 'Horning' was the denunciation of the recalcitrant debtor as a rebel and involved three blasts of the horn by a messenger-at-arms at the market-cross of the 'Head Burgh' of the debtor's domicile or at the market-cross of Edinburgh. Thereafter the debtor was declared an outlaw and the creditor was entitled to proceed to the next stage by 'Letters of Caption' and to have the debtor arrested by the messenger.

Letters of Caption were executed by following an equally elaborate procedure. The messenger-at-arms had to display his blazon bearing the royal arms and was required to touch the debtor with his 'Wand of Peace' which, by the end of the eighteenth century, was an ebony baton six inches long, tipped with silver. At the same time the messenger announced, in the King's name, that the debtor was his prisoner.

From the point of view of the debtor certain loopholes existed. In particular there were restrictions upon the time when Letters of Caption could be executed. While a debtor might be apprehended at any hour of the day or night this rule did not apply to Sunday or a day appointed by Church or State for solemn fast or thanksgiving. Thus it was that Artois was enabled to leave the Abbey Girth on a Sunday.

While the Scottish Sabbath might might provide a temporal shield from the blazon-bearing messenger the precincts of Holyroodhouse provided a territorial refuge.

From the beginning of recorded time sanctuary has had its place in the social order. The sanctuary of the church was recognised in all Christian countries and breach of ecclesiastical sanctuary, while by no means infrequent, as witness the murder of Thomas à Becket in Canterbury or the assassination of Comyn by Bruce in the church of the Convent of the Minories at Dumfries, was a crime demanding expiation of a high order.

The debtor's haven of the Abbey Girth at one time was by no means unique. Another example was the great hospice of Soutra, perched on a lonely rib of the Lammermuirs between the Lothians and Lauderdale, and which gave asylum to the hunted on his journey to the south or north.

The other source of sanctuary sprang from the divinity which by long acceptance hedged a king. Both in England and in Scotland from earliest times the normal operation of the law was suspended in the King's presence. This was in part derived from the view that any crime committed in the royal presence took on a more serious aspect—indeed the 'King's Peace' had an itinerant quality, following majesty like a shadow. The other aspect was that as the King was the fountain of justice so, too, was he the sole arbiter and not to be hampered by rules to which others should conform. In the course of time the special immunities which attached themselves to the royal presence transferred themselves to his dwelling place.

Where ecclesiastical and temporal power combined the right of sanctuary was doubly strong, as at Westminster. When, in 1498, James IV decided to build a castle for his own use in the grounds of the Abbey of the Holy Rood it was the royal aspect which was thenceforth to predominate. Indeed, by that date, the privilege of ecclesiastical sanctuary had become an abuse.

After the Reformation it was in virtue of royal power alone that sanctuary subsisted and by the end of the eighteenth century Holyrood was the only sanctuary remaining in Scotland. Falkland Palace, which had had certain claims, was no longer recognised as such. Even Edinburgh Castle had lost any right to be regarded as a sanctuary. So decided the Court of Session in 1714 when the Governor of the Castle ordered the gates to be shut until a messenger-at-arms who had apprehended the garrison store-master should release his prisoner. Neither was a claim of sanctuary sustained in respect of the old 'Cunzie-House' or mint in the High Street of Edinburgh.

By 1708, however, the sanctuary of the Abbey was formally recognised by the Court, but as a protection against arrest for debt only. The protection did not extend to other offences. At the same time the jurisdiction of the Baillie of the Abbey was acknowledged. The latter was appointed by the Duke of Hamilton who then, as now, held the office of Hereditary Keeper of the Palace. The Baillie had his own Court within the Abbey Girth to decide disputes arising within the sanctuary and he maintained his own prison. While the prison has disappeared the Courtroom remains in the building flanking the west entry to the palace yard.

A description of the sanctuary and its workings as they existed at the time of Artois's arrival is to be found in the lectures which the learned Writer to the Signet, Walter Ross, delivered to his private class of law students in 1783 and 1784.

> Upon the accession of James VI to the throne of England, so fond were we of the least memorial of royalty, that Holyroodhouse continued by consent of the nation, in full possession of its privilege as a sanctuary for civil debts. The Duke of Hamilton, hereditary keeper, or in the language of former times, master of the girth, the only one now in Britain, appoints a baillie under him. This officer has a jurisdiction within the limits of the place, which extends from the Abbey strand and comprehends Arthur's Seat, with the whole grounds and houses within the wall.

Ross explains that in order to obtain the privilege of sanctuary the debtor must enter his name in the book of the deputy baillie and that,

> no person is entitled to the benefit of this sanctuary, after twenty-four hours residence in it, unless his name be so recorded; and this decision is founded upon common sense and expediency, for in many cases, the fact of debtors flying to the Abbey is of the utmost consequence in determining questions; and an extract from this register is the ready and distinct evidence of the fact. . . . The Abbey, however, will afford no asylum to obstinate or fraudulent

> debtors and where this is known or suspected, the Court of Session, upon application of the creditors, will grant a warrant to bring the debtor before them, and commit him to prison, or restore him to the privilege, as his conduct may deserve.

Sir Walter Scott describes the legal position with wit and accuracy in *The Antiquary*. Monkbarns provokes his nephew by saying, 'It is a remarkable thing in this happy country, no man can be legally imprisoned for debt.' When Ochiltree protests Monkbarns replies,

> The truth is, the King is so good as to interfere at the request of the creditor, and to send the debtor his royal command to do him justice within a certain time . . . Well, the man resists and disobeys;—what follows? Why, that he be lawfully and rightfully declared a rebel to our gracious sovereign, whose command he has disobeyed, and that by three blasts of a horn at the market-place of Edinburgh, the metropolis of Scotland. And he is then legally imprisoned, not on account of any civil debt, but because of his ungrateful contempt of the royal mandate.

One has some sympathy with Ochiltree's comment, 'If I had wanted money to pay my debts, I would rather thank the King for sending me some, than to declare me a rebel for not doing what I could not do.'

It is accordingly disappointing to learn that no trace exists of Artois's ever having been Put to the Horn nor having been threatened with Letters of Caption. There is no evidence of his name having been entered in the register of the Baillie Depute. There is, indeed, no record of an effective decree of court having been pronounced against him at the instance of his creditors. Why then did Artois not ignore the restrictions put upon him? It can only be assumed that he, or at least those advising him, felt that the threat of imprisonment was real enough to justify his behaving as if the debts were immediately enforceable.

The sanctuary must have been one of the largest in the world. The Abbey Girth was some four and a half miles in circumference, enclosing the whole of Arthur's Seat. The boundary followed the North shore of Duddingston Loch but excluded the village of Duddingston. From there the boundary ran northwards to Parson's Green where the wall turned west again, and then south west skirting the old Botanical Gardens and the end of Croft an Righ and following the edge of the present-day palace gardens to rejoin the Abbey Mount.

Within the sanctuary were not only the palace itself and the closely packed houses east of Abbeymount, but also the extensive village of St

Ann's which extended from a point not far from the southern flank of the palace to the rising ground at the foot of the Salisbury Crags. In part, at least, its foundations lie beneath the lawns of the present Palace gardens. Thus, by one of those curious turns of history, when Her Majesty, at a Royal Garden Party, proceeds decorously across the grass between the protecting longbows of Her Bodyguard for Scotland, she is treading on the site of the stinking tenements once occupied by the 'Abbey Lairds', perhaps even that in which Thomas de Quincey sought forgetfulness in opium. We have to imagine Artois and his little court living in unsavoury proximity to much less fortunate debtors.

Worse for Artois and his courtiers was a stretch of open ground called St Ann's Yard. Henry Courtoy, Keeper of the Chapel Royal, in his guide to the Abbey and Palace of Holyrood written in the 1820s, tells us that 'the portion lying next to the Palace, almost under its very windows, is a most abominable nuisance'. He spares us nothing:

> Here an artificial marsh is created by stopping up the course of the common sewer of the city, which is conducted in this direction to the sea, and by spreading over the surface the contents of the sewer. Most odiferous is the scent of this beauteous meadow in the heats of summer, when its rich rankness of corrupting animal and vegetable excrementation is steaming from its fetid surface, and sending its grateful perfume to the adjoining Palace—truly 'a dainty dish to set before a King.'

An early nineteenth century pamphleteer has said of the sanctuary that it was the 'tomb of credit'. As the writer put it, 'he or she who once gets the bush-fighting plan, of skirmishing from old Holyrood and retiring upon its privilege, will no more be trusted'. On the other hand, for the debtor who had no immediate hope of settling with his creditors but had a pittance left or who could rely on the charity of family and friends, the Abbey provided a place of residence incomparably better than the debtors' jail.

A near enough contemporary picture of life within the sanctuary is given in Courtoy's Guide. It is colourful enough to quote at some length:

> Once within the Girth, you will find yourself surrounded with habitations erst occupied by the nobles of Scotland, attendants of the royal Scottish Court, but now by keepers of comfortable lodgings for the Abbey Lairds; the ground-floors fronting the street having been in wonderfully numerous instances converted into petty taverns. Peeping from the windows and doors of these hostelries, if in winter, and if in summer, lounging about the street with a

wistful eye to the Canongate side of the strand, or reclining by twos and threes on benches in front of the change-houses, you will discover a variety of shabby-genteel-devil-me-care-looking personages.

Courtoy continues:

These worthies, have all passed the *ruby*-con: they have had their vicissitudes of good and bad fortune, their term of wrecking argosies, of ruinous speculations, of accommodation bills returned upon them, of prodigality, of dissipation, of the broken spirit, or of the hairbreadth 'scapes from the fangs of the law. Their cup of the ills that flesh is heir to is descending to the bitter and muddy lees. They know this; with only an occasional sigh over the remembrance of the past, they may be found together nightly, like the heroes of Woolwich or Chelsea, laid up in local fellowship, fighting their battles o'er again, with sole remaining solace of the tankard and pipe.

St Ann's seems to have housed the longer term resident.

If you have sufficient reason to suppose that you will have to locate, as the Americans say, for any pretty-considerable period, you may pass on through the palace-yard, and, before you reach the park, you will find on your right another cluster of antique domicils, full of 'lodgings to let,' and varying in their external appearance and interior accommodation from the tolerable, to the 'most (in)tolerable and not to be endured.'

At last, having ransacked the 'lodgings to let', both in the main street and alleys behind, and also in the more retired territory spoken of; made choice, and having arranged for the payment of from 3s. to 6s., as you and your landlady can agree upon, as the weekly rent of your little apartment, with a bed in it or off it; and having, like a student come to attend college, unpacked and laid out your small assortment of linen and books, including the woful ledger, you may sit down at your ease during twenty-four hours, for you are as yet in safety 'for this night only' to study the law of this land of liberty.

Thus, while within the walls of the palace itself, Monsieur lived in relative comfort and while he had the whole of the King's Park at his disposal—he could even shoot snipe in Hunter's Bog—it would be a mistake to imagine his little court living in isolation. Artois's sanctuary was shared with the floating debris of Scottish and English society, those neither poor enough to be forced to the nether depths nor rich enough to escape the confines of debt. The lodgings of the Abbey Lairds abutted on the palace and in his sundry sorties Artois rubbed shoulders with those whose lot he shared.

CHAPTER 7

Comings and Goings of the Emigrés

Monsieur remained confined to the sanctuary of Holyroodhouse until the summer of 1798, when for the reasons given later, he regained his freedom of movement. The picture which emerges from the memoirs and letters of his period of captivity is of Artois's sitting impotently on the periphery of events, vainly seeking to alter the mixture simmering in the cauldron of Europe. As regards the domestic scene, there remained around him a small inner company of the faithful, for the most part politically inept. This Artois himself recognised in a report destined for Louis XVIII: 'In the small group which Monsieur has retained close to his person, he has not met talent of a superior quality having the spirit and the experience capable of directing important matters.'

There was also a larger group which came and went, bearing the news, usually bad, of the wider world and departing with instruction and exhortation.

Socially the *émigrés* kept a low profile, the early levees apart. Vaudreuil in February 1796 wrote to his father:

> The Scottish nobility is full of kindness, hospitality and good manners, and parties, balls and concerts are not wanting but it is better to keep a certain distance, following the example of our august Prince. We are in bed every night before midnight and we feel the better for it.

This was in part due to the poor health of Louise de Polastron, and Artois's letters to Vaudreuil contain regular reports on her condition. 'My friend has recently had a serious inflammation from which she has suffered greatly; but, thanks be to God, she is very well at present', wrote Artois to Vaudreuil in September 1796. There were many ups and downs, typical of the progress of consumption. For example, two years later, Louise, herself, was more confident:

> Believe it or not we have had for the last fortnight a superb summer by the standards of this country; I feel marvellous. Truly, I go out every day, either

> on foot or on horseback, and the bitter drug which the doctor has given me is doing a power of good. So, for the moment I am in splendid form and even putting on some weight. All the same I fear that we pay a price for this lovely weather.

Nothing, in the long run, however, could abate the progress of her disease.

There were, of course, exceptions to the quiet routine. Artois and his entourage were frequent visitors to the Buccleuchs at Dalkeith Palace. Angoulême, in particular, formed an affectionate relationship with the Duchess which was later reflected in a long series of letters when once more he resumed his vagrant life. These letters, preserved in the Buccleuch archives and written in charmingly fractured English, make it clear that the Duchess and her family represented for Angoulême the domestic stability which he had never known. On 2 November 1797 he writes to her, from Blankenburg in the Hartz Mountains where he had rejoined Louis XVIII, thanking the Duchess for the purchase of a lottery ticket. He adds,

> Your Grace can see that I use of her kindness for me in being with her upon the same footing as you was my own mother. I hope that you will excuse, madam, the liberty that I take in telling to you with the greatest sincerity, that I have and shall have for life the sentiments and affection of a son for your Grace.

An early arrival in Edinburgh, and one who was to play a critical role for the rest of Artois's life, was the future Cardinal Latil. It was he who, after the death of Louise de Polastron in 1804, secured Artois's adherence to the ultra-clerical cabal which dominated the French government in the 1820s and who was in large measure responsible for the intransigence of Artois which precipitated the Revolution of July 1830. Cardinal Latil, it was, who crowned Artois as King of France and Navarre at Rheims in 1824, again accompanied his patron to Edinburgh during the second exile of 1830 and who, in 1836, administered to him the last sacrament in far-off Goritz in present-day Slovenia.

At the time of Monsieur's arrival in Edinburgh there was a small Catholic church in Blackfriars Wynd, and initially Sunday Mass was there attended by Artois and his companions. This, however, soon changed. The story is told by Madame de Boigne:

After his arrival at Holyrood, the Comte d'Artois, who was anything but a religious man, was greatly troubled by the zeal of the Scottish Catholics to provide him with masses and services. At some great festival their forethought obliged him to go twenty miles in order to spend five or six hours in the chapel of a neighbouring nobleman. Tired by this imposition, he wished to have an almoner. Mme de Polastron wrote to Mme de Lage, and asked her to find a priest to say Mass, of a social standing sufficiently low to exclude him from the apartments, the Comte's intention being that he should take his meals with the valet de chambre. Mme de Lage applied to M. de Sabran, who said, 'I have just what you want, a priest who is the son of my concièrge. He is young, not bad looking, not difficult in any way and you will have no trouble with him.' The proposal was explained to the Abbé Latil. He accepted joyfully, and was packed off by coach to Edinburgh where he was installed upon the terms proposed.

Thus the modest priest placed his foot on the ladder of advancement leading to a Dukedom of France and the papal ring.

The immediate consequence of the arrival of the Abbé Latil's arrival in Edinburgh was the establishment of a chapel at the end of the long gallery, where, as Francis Steuart has observed, a guidebook of 1818 points out that Mass was said without the smallest opposition from either the clergy or people of Edinburgh.

It is not to be supposed that the *émigrés* were always united amongst themselves. Louise de Polastron was at the heart of much bickering and affected by it all. Her letters to Sophie de Lage de Volude are full of the depression brought about by her failing health and by the 'poisoned gossip'—*commerages envenimés*—which surrounded her. As always, should Artois hesitate to be more active in the royal interest, she was blamed for being over-protective. Madame de Boigne's tart comment was not untypical. Louise loved Artois, she wrote, 'passionately, but not to his greater glory. The less than honourable role played by the Prince during the Revolution was due to the influence which she exercised.' Certainly, any criticism of Artois, however justified, distressed Louise, as when, on one occasion, he was in her hearing unfavourably compared with the Duc de Bourbon. The Duc, it was said, was as ready to make the gesture of joining the resistance in the Vendée as Artois was reluctant. In its turn, gossip riposted that the Duc de Bourbon had so far made no move, being anchored to London by the charms of the young Comtesse de Vaudreuil.

Both more serious and tragic was the quarrel that arose between the essentially moderate Abbé de Montesquiou, who was later mistrusted by the royalists as being too close to Talleyrand, and the Comte de Sérent, the elder son of the Duc de Sérent, and who had been an aide-de camp to Artois on the Ile d'Yeu. The former had accused the latter of attempting to persuade Lord William Wyndham, Secretary of State in Pitt's cabinet, to reject certain requests which Artois had made. Madame de Lage deplored the misunderstanding which had separated the two men 'each so well-endowed to befriend the other.'

'I do not know,' wrote Madame de Lage on 4 June 1796,

> who has the greater sparkle and knowledge and who has the greater gift of persuasion. I was all the same astonished by the vivacity of the Abbé on that occasion for although he defends his friends so well and with such skill it is by his calm and gentle manner and with attention so that he recovers ground foot by foot, skipping skilfully over matters which he cannot excuse or justify. Add to that his spirit, the clearness of his ideas, his power of memory and an eloquence which pierces the soul. He can, in truth, make you take his part by the interest he arouses even if in the beginning you had no taste for it. The Comte de Sérent has the same manner in argument. He, too, knows how to listen and reply without the least animosity, and he has such a talent for making you believe that you had already thought for yourself the point that he is making that it is impossible not to be charmed by him.

Alas, after this public quarrel, Edinburgh could no longer contain them both, and with characteristic gallantry the Comte de Sérent set out to join the insurgents in France.

It seems certain that the Comte de Sérent was the person referred to by Pryse Lockhart Gordon:

> I formed a great intimacy with an interesting and highly educated young nobleman of high birth, who being desirous to learn English, often came to breakfast with me to get a lesson, and his progress was astonishing; but this promising youth was called away to fight the battles of his friends in the Vendée, and fell in that heroic venture.

It must have been a short-lived intimacy. The Fonds Bourbon at the Quai d'Orsay in Paris contain a moving letter from Sérent in Jersey to the Comte d'Artois in Edinburgh, dated March 1796, which ends with the words

> It is with lively satisfaction that I see from here the ship in which I shall embark in half an hour's time to cross to France and I take up my pen to wish you the last farewell which your humble servant will address to you on British soil. This evening, I hope, I shall be in your homeland.

Last farewell indeed. Less than two months later Artois received, again from Jersey, the news of Sérent's death in the marshes, not of the Vendée, but of Brittany. To add to the old Duke's distress, Sérent's younger brother was killed in the same skirmish. Writing to Vaudreuil on 7 May 1796 Artois says, 'I expect his poor father this evening; I hope that I can ease his grief by sharing it.'

In September 1796 there arrived by the same post-chaise three very different characters. The first to be mentioned, since he had organised the journey, even if he had not paid for his fellow passengers, was the Baron de Roll. He is an intriguing figure and is to be found in the background at every turn of events over a considerable period. In 1791, for example, he is the accredited messenger in the Royalist cause between the Emperor in Vienna and Catherine the Great at St Petersburg, and again, in 1793, we find him acting as Artois's private emissary to Prussia. He was born in 1743, a Swiss, and was rich enough, even as late as the 1790s, to raise a regiment which bore his name and in the service of which the young Henri-Louis de Polastron ended his life in 1804, dead of yellow fever at Gibraltar. At Holyrood the Baron was important enough to have a room named after him in Young, Trotter and Hamilton's accounts. As a man, however, no picture of him emerges from the many passing references. We know nothing of his appearance, his likes and dislikes, and little of his personality. He is a key figure who never emerges from his grey twilight. One of the few comments comes from Lady Jermingham: 'M. de Montyon says "*C'etait un Honnete Homme, mais de toute nullite*". However, a sincerely attached friend to an unfortunate Prince is always of some consequence.' The same feeling is echoed by Lady Louisa Stuart. 'An honest Swiss' is all she has to say. He died at Tonbridge on 28 August 1830 having lived just long enough to see the 'unfortunate Prince' leave France for his second exile.

The second passenger in the post-chaise was the Abbé Edgeworth, the Irish priest who had attended Louis XVI on the scaffold. Edgeworth had only very recently reached England, having spent the previous twenty-six months hidden in France, including twelve, when he dared not leave his room. For Artois it was a sad encounter. Writing to Vaudreuil, who was temporarily in London, Artois tells him to be sure to see the Abbé on his return, and speaks warmly of his 'courage, fidelity and devotion'.

The third passenger was the painter, Pierre Danloux. Danloux had been a pupil of Lepicié and Vien and was a draughtsman of great skill. By the time the Revolution began he was in considerable demand as a portraitist by the world of Versailles and had, indeed, been commissioned by

Artois. With his wife and family he had escaped in 1795 and quickly re-established himself in London. In June 1796 the Comte de Damas had arrived in London bearing a letter from Louise de Polastron asking that Danloux should visit Edinburgh to paint Monsieur, since the latter had been displeased with the efforts of another painter whose identity we do not know. Danloux had some trouble in finding enough ready cash to make the journey, but once this difficulty was overcome and the Baron de Roll was ready to travel, they set out on 3 September.

The journey was uneventful, and Danloux, according to his wife's journal, was pleased with his reception and found that a modest lodging had been reserved for him by Madame de Polastron while he ate with Monsieur's almoner and physician.

Danloux worked fast. By 15 September Artois was able to say to Vaudreuil, 'I have at last the portrait which I now send. In all faith it is the best, and I give it to you with all my heart. Danloux has made another which people think well of and say that it should be engraved: you will get it in London.'

Engraved it was by Andrea Freschi, an Italian who had long worked in London, with the inscription, 'After the original picture in the possession of M. le Comte Francois Des Cars.'

Danloux put his time in Edinburgh to good use. In her journal for 27 November Madame Danloux notes:

> He tells me that he has finished the portrait of the two princes—that is, Artois and Angoulême—and painted on a small scale one of the young Polastron. He has on hand the portraits of Lord Adam Gordon, the Duc de Maillé, the Duc de Sérent and Mme de Polastron, to be followed by two copies of those of the princes. All this gives me much pleasure.

There are, or were, two charming portraits of Louise de Polastron. The one, a miniature, is signed by the minor artist, Louise de Beaurepaire. Louise de Polastron's hands are concealed in a large fur muff while her long hair and the ostrich feathers in her hat blow in the cold wind. The painter has sought to create something gay for the pleasure of Monsieur, but while the smile is captivating the eyes are tired and little imagination is required to sense that consumption was already beginning to take its toll. It was at one time thought that the larger of the two was the painting to which Madame Danloux refers. Wind-blown locks and a fur muff are certainly consistent with Edinburgh in November, but the Beaurepaire miniature was certainly painted in France. As regards the Danloux, Artois, sometime after the death of Louise, and perhaps feeling that he could no longer live with it, gave the painting to Madame de Gontaut, in whose family it remained, at least until the beginning of this century; but efforts to find its whereabouts have proved unavailing.

Louise's son, Henri-Louis de Polastron, was aged eleven when Danloux painted his portrait. To judge from the indifferent reproduction of it in Portalis's book on Danloux he was a good-looking boy who possessed his fair share of impertinence. According to Robert Chambers he used to attend the dancing lessons given by Signor Rossignoli, who lived in Baillie Fyfe's Close, and, 'he was in love with about two score Scottish young ladies at once. He used to wait at the bottom of the stairs, in order to catch and kiss them, his fellow pupils, one by one as they descended—his valet assisting him by holding them, till they were all dispatched'.

To revert to Pierre Danloux: While he was delighted with the success of his commissions and the praise bestowed upon his work, he had little time for the company which Artois kept. In a letter to his wife he reports, 'the Prince is good but feeble and his entourage very bad. His son is an imbecile, stupid and obstinate and everyone who is here are servile courtiers.' He tells his wife of a petulant quarrel between the Duc d'Angoulême and the Comte de Rebourguil, who appears to have acted as a general factotum to the household, and on his return to London recounts that, 'while the Prince is excellent, all those who surround him are intriguers, rascals (*fripons*) or thoughtless; everyone looked after his own interests and there was not the least order in the household.'

Among the many arrivals and departures there was one departure which for Artois and Louise represented the end of a long companionship. The Duc de Polignac and the Comtesse Diane left for Russia where they had been promised asylum by Catherine the Great. Unfortunately for the Polignacs the Empress died shortly after their arrival and was succeeded by the unpredictable Czar Paul. Their difficult position is reflected in a letter of February 1797 from Artois to the Comtesse Diane:

> M. de Rivière was charged with a letter to the late Empress which he will surely have delivered to her successor; what is more, in writing to that prince on the occasion of his accession I have specially commended to him the Duc de Polignac and his family. But, as I do not wish to raise your hopes too high, I will say frankly, *ma bonne mère*, I can do no more at the moment. If the reply of the new Emperor is favourable I will press for something to be done quickly; if the reply is less cordial I will perhaps find other ways.

In the same letter Artois gives us a rare glimpse into his inner feelings:

> The sky remains as stormy as ever but we must not lack courage and you may be sure, sure indeed, that it is not in the deserts of the Ukraine nor in the neighbourhood of the North Pole that we will find again our happiness but only when we are once again at home in the France of yesteryear.

The last few words are particularly telling in the original—*dans l'ancienne France*. Unlike his much wiser elder brother, Louis XVIII, Artois was incapable of recognising the inevitability of change. For him *l'ancien régime* was the true and only faith.

All, in the end, went well for the Polignacs. The Duc de Polignac was well received into the Russian service and was amply endowed with a starostie or feudal lordship in the Ukraine, between the Dnieper and the Dniester, and the considerable income that went with it. Holyrood rejoiced at their good fortune, as a joint letter by Artois and Louise de Polastron bears witness. Artois concludes, 'do not speak of final separation'—but final separation it was. The Duc de Polignac died at St Petersburg in 1817, predeceased, it seems, by his sister.

The good fortune of the Polignacs serves to underline the poverty they left behind. The Comte d'Artois was not ill provided for in the palace itself, and neither was Angoulême, so long as he was in residence. Monsieur had his allowance of £500 per month from the British Government and Angoulême his, of £300, but with so many calls upon their generosity these subventions did not go far. We have seen from Madame de Gontaut how his entertaining had to be restricted, and the same was even more apparent in the case of his followers.

Louise de Polastron puts it graphically in a letter to Blimonette:

> You would be astonished if you knew the trouble which I take to be an unworthy miser, for such little details are no part of my character. You must realise that we have all changed. No carriage, only two entrees provided by Monsieur, few guests. As for me I can only spend a fixed amount on this and a fixed amount on that and it is little enough for each. Henri [her cook] complains. I tell him, 'There is no argument. I cannot do otherwise. If you can manage, well and good. If not, cut back until you get there.'

Louise adds, 'He retreats pensively'.

The case of Vaudreuil well illustrates the unaccustomed effects of poverty. Writing from Edinburgh to his mother in April 1796 about his temporary return to London he asks her to buy second-hand kitchen equipment and linen, and in August we find him seeking help from Artois, who is constrained to reply that he has only been able to assist with difficulty, and that his charity must not be divulged to anyone: 'I do not like this but it is necessary for you and me.'

On his return to Edinburgh in November, Vaudreuil, again writing to his mother, tells her:

> We have found a house which costs us four pounds a month. We have only ten pounds a month in all and for all. Monsieur adds to our dinner two dishes which he sends from the chateau. I had indeed hoped for something more but this hope must be abandoned since he cannot meet his own household expenses. To tell the truth I do not know how I shall manage and my head is turned.

Indeed the decline of Vaudreuil's fortunes was the more dramatic since he had originally been better off than many of his compatriots. The substantial revenue from the sugar plantations in San Domingo owned by his family had made him among the richer of the *émigrés*. The negro revolt under Toussaint Louverture threatened all this, and Vaudreuil's letters are full of anxiety concerning the affairs of the island, the attempt to suppress the rising and the eventual evacuation of the island by its British garrison.

In true *émigré* tradition recourse was had to the sale of the more desirable forms of moveable property, in the case of Vaudreuil, what remained of his collection of pictures. There was one difficulty—the pictures were still in France and history does not record that he ever took delivery. Probably not, as Vaudreuil's poverty remained chronic. Once again to his mother, this time in August 1798, he says: 'I shall sell my piano to buy a little time. It is all that I have left to sacrifice and it is truly a sacrifice since Pauline [his sister-in-law] accompanies my wife who is making progress. We shall sing no more.'

Poverty did not impede the tide of comings and goings. The most important departure and arrival during Monsieur's enforced stay in Holyrood were those of the Duc d'Angoulême and the Duc de Berry. The former finally left Edinburgh in March 1797 for Hamborg, then still a free port in the Prussian sphere of influence. From there his destination was Blankenburg in the Hartz mountains, which formed part of the Duchy of Brunswick and where Louis XVIII was in residence as a guest of the Duke. The Duc de Berry, who had been serving with the army of the Prince de Condé, did not arrive in Edinburgh until March or April 1798 and left again the following September. The movement of the Princes and the political preoccupations of Artois and his followers are best seen against a brief description of what was happening on the mainland of Europe. This is reserved for a later chapter. Here it is enough to say that it would be wrong to imagine the *émigrés* as wholly concerned with the minutiae of life. They were deeply concerned with events abroad, even if there was little they could do to influence them. Artois, at least, remained invincibly optimistic. 'Do not doubt it—we shall find again our much loved home [*nous retrouverons nos doux pénates*] after some necessary thrusts of the sabre; and a long period of happiness will blot out the unhappy past. This prophecy is much better founded than those of Nostradamus,' he wrote in a letter to Blimonette.

Since, however, this chapter is largely concerned with personal relations it may fittingly end with a very domestic scene—amateur theatricals in honour of Monsieur's birthday. The time is August 1798 and the young Duke de Berry was of the company. Indeed one suspects that he did much to liven an otherwise doleful assembly. The Duc de Berry 'loved music and music we had', says Madame de Gontaut. Here is Vaudreuil's account given in a letter to his mother:

> Yesterday we gave to Monsieur a small entertainment of which he knew nothing as he would not have agreed to it for reasons of prudence and circumspection. Accordingly he was led to the bedroom of his son who the evening before had been a trifle unwell. He there found a theatre, formed with screens and crossed curtains, lit with candles which normally served the billiard table. The orchestra consisted of Pauline on her own, playing the piano-forte: the audience was composed of valets, chamber-maids and other servants. The play then began and very good it was, the little comedy *Le Sourd* and the proverb *Le Veuf*, truly very well and amusingly done. Monsieur laughed a lot, something which seldom happens, and for us it was a real pleasure to see him for a moment distracted from his cares. My wife, because of her present plump figure [she was pregnant again] played the part of Mme Le Gras, landlady of an inn at Avignon. She imitated the Provencal accent marvelously . . . M. le Duc de Berry played the role of a rich bourgeois, de Doliban, and was dressed up as well as can be imagined. The whole affair was perfect and I shall settle the entire bill for a guinea. Beyond doubt one can call it an innocent pleasure. Perhaps evil tongues would give it the high-sounding name of a fête; what can one do? It reminds me of all the trouble we had when we wanted the children to act Cinderella and that without costing anything. So keep all this to yourself, I beg of you. If anyone mentions it to you, you know what to say because I have given you the exact truth.

All this is a far cry from the theatre of the Petit Trianon.

CHAPTER 8

The First Departure

Artois's confinement came to an end during the summer of 1798—two-and-a-half years after he had first crossed the threshold of Holyroodhouse. His freedom is attested by an entry in the library records of Dalkeith Palace for 6 July 1798. 'Monsieur' and his party, which included the Duc de Berry, were weighed on the library scales and the weights duly recorded. 'S.A.R. Monsieur' tops the list at nearly 13½ stones, while Berry is just over 11. Others present were 'le Marquis de Polignac', 'le Ct. Frans. Descars', 'le Duc de Maillé' and the 'le Victe. de Vaudreuil'. Apart from the oddity of the occasion the date is significant; 6 July 1798 was a Friday, and Artois evidently had felt able to leave his sanctuary.

Various explanations have been given of how this came about.

According to Madame de Gontaut, 'the upright and skilful men of the law employed by our Prince at length succeeded in setting at liberty the noble prisoner of Holyrood as there was no proof sufficient to justify the demand for such enormous sums.' 'Philo Scotus', *alias* Phillip Barrington Ainslie of Pilton, tells us:

> I may here mention that the law agent employed by the creditors of the Comte d'Artois was Mr. C. Tait (father of the present most estimable Bishop of London), who made arrangements with the Prince as enabled him, ere long, to leave the bounds of the sanctuary of Holyrood—which, although very extensive, including the King's Park and the beautiful mountain and lake scenery of Arthur's Seat, as well as Duddingston Loch, was yet but a prison, and felt as such by the Prince.

The estimable son of Mr Tait was subsequently to become Archbishop of Canterbury, an achievement as yet unequalled among the progeny of Edinburgh solicitors.

The *Gentleman's Magazine*, also, speaks of an arrangement having been made with Artois's creditors. It is Madame de Boigne who comes nearest to the truth when she asserts that the liberation of Artois was due to the passing of an Act of Parliament that 'decided that arrest was illegal in the case of debts contracted abroad'. This was the Aliens Act of 1798 which, for the duration of the current hostilities, gave immunity in the British courts to those who had entered into any obligations overseas.

The primary purpose of the Aliens Act was to require the registration of Aliens and to control their movements in the interests of national security. Section 9, however, provided that 'Aliens abiding in this Kingdom, having quitted their respective Countries by reason of any Revolution or troubles in France . . . shall not be liable to be arrested . . . by reason of any debt' contracted abroad. As will be seen, the time limit placed on the immunity, 'six months after the conclusion of a general peace', became important a few years later.

Artois did not immediately abandon Holyrood, which remained his base until August 1799. He seems to have made full use of his newly acquired freedom and, again according to Madame de Gontaut, embarked on a round of visits to thank the 'illustrious chiefs of the Scottish clans' for their kindness to him while restricted to the Abbey Girth.

During June and July 1799 Artois was in London and engaged in discussion with various members of the Government. Rumour had it that he was seeking the leadership of yet another assault on the French coast, this time with the aid of twenty thousand Swiss mercenaries. If there were any truth in this it was a proposition not encouraged by the British Government. None the less Artois had decided to remove himself to London, the better to pursue his schemes. On a brief return to Edinburgh he issued, on 5 August 1799, the following letter of farewell to the Lord Provost and Magistrates:

> I am forced, by circumstances touching the true service of the King, my brother, to leave the country where, during the whole time of my residence, I have received unvaryingly the most distinguished marks of attention and respect. I would reproach myself if I went away without expressing to the respective magistrates and through them to all the inhabitants, the feeling of gratitude with which my heart is filled, for the noble manner in which they have seconded the generous hospitality of his Britannic Majesty. I hope one day to be able, in happier times, to make my sentiments on this subject known, and to explain them more fully. With the sentiments which are inspired by you, and the sincere assurance which alone the time permits to offer you, I sign,
>
> CHARLES PHILIPPE.

'Circumstances touching the true service of the King, my brother.' What were they?

During the first period of Artois's residence at Holyrood, from 1796 to 1799, there had been substantial and frequent changes in the situation on the mainland of Europe. His first year in Edinburgh saw the downfall and execution of Robespierre in July 1796 and the replacement of his regime by the Directory. The Directory, in its turn, embraced a bewildering series of changes among the Directors prompted by frequent *coups d'états* or attempted *coups d'états*. This was the period of Napoleon's rise to power following his spectacular conquest of Northern Italy. The campaign ended in 1797 with the Treaty of Campoformio which created a new French dominated Cisalpine Republic and granted to Austria the greater part of Venetian territory. Included in the Cisalpine Republic were the possessions of Artois's father-in-law, the King of Sardinia. The Directory lasted only until 1799, to be succeeded by the Consulate with General Bonaparte as first consul. Henceforth it was Napoleon Bonaparte, rather than the abstract French Republic, who became the target of royalist animosity. Napoleon's success in Northern Italy made it imperative that Louis XVIII, who had, at first, quartered himself with the Prince de Condé's army east of the Rhine, should find securer quarters. These were offered by the Duke of Brunswick at Blankenburg, and it was there that Louis XVIII summoned the Duc d'Angoulême to join him in the spring of 1797. Their stay was to be relatively short. Prussia, on hearing the news of the Treaty of Campoformio, feared that it might be exposed to attack by French troops no longer required in Italy. 'The peace of the Emperor has greatly altered all my schemes,' wrote Angoulême to the Duchess of Buccleuch in May 1797. However, he and Louis XVIII remained at Blankenburg for the remainder of that year, despite 'the same incertitude upon the dispositions peaceable or hostile of the Emperor', as Angoulême put it to the Duchess, and the departure of the Prince de Condé's army to enter the service of Russia. In November 1797 Louis XVIII and the Duc d'Angoulême were joined at Blankenburg by the Duc de Berry, awaiting a British frigate to reach Cuxhaven in order to take Berry to join Artois at Holyrood. 'I can't give to my brother a too favourable idea of the hospitality and high sentiments of the Scottish Nation and of what he must expect to find at Edinburgh,' wrote Angoulême.

Berry in fact had to wait until February for his frigate, the Royal Navy having, no doubt, more pressing commitments, but by this time Louis XVIII was under peremptory notice to quit Blankenburg. Fortunately the Tsar, Paul I, in one of his more lucid and non-francophobic moments—it has been said that to wear French fashions at St Petersburg was the equivalent of suicide—had offered to Louis XVIII his castle at Mitau in

Courland, now Jelgava, a few miles from Riga in present-day Latvia. Edinburgh was able to follow the horrors of the winter journey to the Baltic through Angoulême's letters to the Duchess of Buccleuch: 'We have seen several times twenty horses at the same time to the King's carriage and almost always twelve'. In the end Mittau, despite its remoteness and severe climate, turned out to be a pleasant enough refuge, and there for the moment we leave Louis VIII and the Duc d'Angoulême.

The Duc de Berry, in the meanwhile, had arrived in Scotland where he passed the summer and enlivened the Palace of Holyroodhouse. Again the Buccleuchs were the soul of hospitality. 'In every letter that I received from him he speaks with the highest gratitude of the attentions and goodness which are paid to him at Dalkeith', wrote Angoulême to the Duchess on 12 May 1798.

One person, at the end of 1797, had made the journey from Edinburgh to Blankenburg and back again. This was the faithful Comte d'Escars, and his mission was to improve the deteriorating relations between Artois and Louis XVIII. Apart from the difference in temperament between the two brothers there had been disagreement over the distribution of funds which Louis XVIII had received from Russia, and it was finally agreed that each should have his own zone of influence. Despite the disasters of Quiberon and Ile d'Yeu the royalist cause was not wholly obliterated. Pockets of resistance to the French Republic remained in Normandy, Britanny and the Vendée. Louis XVIII agreed to recognise Artois's responsibility for these areas, and thus it was that to him the leaders of the *chouannerie* in these provinces turned. Many were the emissaries who made the difficult journey to Holyrood from the west of France only to depart with a baggage-load of unfulfilled promises.

The Comtesse de Boigne describes one such visit in October 1797 by the brother of General de Frotté, who commanded the resistance in Normandy and who sought, in vain, Artois's presence on the French mainland.

> 'It is not possible to prevaricate—war alone, Monseigneur, can save us! The west requires a prince and money and both together.' Artois is shaken and moved by this prospect. Immediately his 'Council' get together—that is to say the eight or ten persons including Vaudreuil, the bishop of Arras, [de Conzié], the Baron de Roll and the Chevalier de Puységur. They take a strong line and attack Frotté with questions; 'How many *valets de chambre*, cooks, surgeons will Monsieur have?' asks the Baron de Roll.
>
> 'One moment please. I am the Captain of the Guard of Monsieur, the Comte

> d'Artois and responsible to the King for Monseigneur's safety. Does M. de Frotté assure us that Monseigneur will run no risk?'
>
> 'My answer is that there are a hundred thousand men prepared to die before a hair of his head is harmed. I can say no more.'
>
> 'I turn to you gentlemen,' replies the Baron de Roll. 'Is that a sufficient guarantee of the safety of Monseigneur! Can I possibly agree to it?'

Madame de Boigne is using her imagination but the tenor of her description is accurate enough.

The following year Bourmont, later the conqueror of Algiers and a fellow exile in Edinburgh in 1830, joined the insurgents in the Vendée and made the same proposal to Artois, only to have it rejected as nebulous. With perhaps more reason Artois rebuffed the request of the Comte de Puisaye, 'Come, Monseigneur, and place yourself at the head of men prepared to sacrifice their life for you.' Puisaye had been the architect of the catastrophe of Quiberon and had few supporters, French or British. To him Artois replied, 'I cannot for the moment authorise any insurrection in the Western provinces. I will provoke one by my presence, and I will not answer to posterity for blood which I have spilled in vain'.

A much more sympathetic character than the foregoing was Georges Cadoudal, universally known as 'Georges'. Large and jolly, the son of a miller, he had established himself as one of the leaders of the resistance in the Vendée. At the end of 1797 or the beginning of 1798 he made the same journey to Holyrood and he too was rebuffed. 'Georges', however was indefatigable and Artois had not seen or heard the last of him.

The other event of importance at this time was the marriage between the Duc d'Angoulême and his cousin, the daughter of Louis XVI, Madame Royale, which after protracted negotiations eventually took place at Mittau in June 1799. It is often pictured as a loveless marriage, but this is not correct. In his letters to the Duchess of Buccleuch Angoulême expresses real enthusiasm for the match and a contemporary account describes the bride's vivacity and charm at the wedding. It was a marriage that was to endure for 45 years of mutual support and loyalty. Inevitably, with hindsight, it was a childless marriage. The Duc D'Angoulême was a celibate Bourbon, unlike his brother the Duc de Berry, who was a libidinous Bourbon, and the traumatic events of Madame Royale's childhood must have taken their psychological toll. The dynastic result, however, was that the future of the Bourbon line lay with the progeny of the Duc de Berry.

Artois tried to attend the marriage at Mittau or, at least, said that he had tried, but that the British government would not make possible the journey.

Finally, for the time being, on 8 August 1799, the *Edinburgh Evening Courant* announced that 'M. le Compte d'Artois with his suite set off for England', and soon after he was installed in London at 46 Baker Street, with Louise de Polastron less than two hundred yards away at 18 Thayer Street. The daily round of whist could recommence.

'The true service of the King, my brother?' On 7 September 1799 the official journals announced that Monsieur had postponed indefinitely his departure for the Continent owing to an attack of haemorrhoids.

CHAPTER 9

'Tiresome and Odd'?: The Emigrés' View of the Scots

By 1796 there was, of course, already a substantial *émigré* population in London and the south of England. Relatively few, however, had ventured farther north, and on the part of the majority who remained in southern England there was little desire to become an integral part of the community which had shown them real, if sometimes reluctant, hospitality. If this generalisation seems uncharitable it is one accepted by the French themselves. For example, in his *Histoire de l'Emigration*, Ghislain de Diesbach writes:

> There was not on the part of the French, be they *grands seigneurs* or country squires, modest priests or dignatories of the Church, any real desire to assimilate themselves, any effort to learn the local language nor the slightest attempt to comply with local custom which seemed to them tiresome and odd.

There were obvious exceptions. Poverty was a great leveller and there are many stories of the straits to which the *émigrés* were reduced and the stratagems which they were forced to adopt. The true heroines were, as often as not, the wives, ever ready to engage in trade which their husbands spurned as unbefitting a gentleman. In London, indeed, so great was the influx of impecunious French that relief schemes, both publicly and privately funded, had to be created.

In Edinburgh, Artois and those around him were a case apart, although we have seen that they too had their money problems. They were made welcome by the aristocracy even if, following Artois's example, they restricted their enjoyment of the social round. Nevertheless, the coterie seems to have shared the prevailing attitude of being uninterested in their surroundings. There is no evidence of any social contact between Holyrood and the Universities nor with any of Edinburgh's increasingly influential professional classes. The Faculty of Advocates had opened their famous library to Artois but no use seems ever to have been made of this privilege. Not that one would have expected it of Artois, but some of the courtiers were men and women of greater intellectual endowment.

Poverty certainly played a part in erecting barriers. It was difficult to cut even a modest dash in Edinburgh when the piano had to be sold to provide subsistence, but there was more to it than that. The court at Versailles had thought of themselves as the centre of existence—only those to whom it was anathema, like Louis XVI, could find interests elsewhere. In exile and day-dreaming it was to their former existence that they returned. We find Vaudreuil in Edinburgh, beset with problems, thinking about the family estate in the Languedoc and planning to live there and 'to embellish it and to make happy its faithful inhabitants'. Unconsciously, perhaps, he was compensating for his lack of action at a time when he might have taken positive steps. The Vaudreuil chateau with its medieval towers still crowns a pine-clad hilltop in the Haut-Garonne, east of Carcassonne, at the point where the *Montagnes Noires* meet the plain of Toulouse. A local guide-book refers to its 'sleeping beauty' quality which is perhaps no more than a euphemism for neglect and—it may be too strong a word—the hypocrisy of Vaudreuil's Edinburgh vision.

To see Edinburgh through French eyes at this period it is necessary to find someone outside those comprising the Artois circle, and who, unlike them, was interested in the world about him. Fortunately, one such exists, Captain Louis de Boisgelin. Louis de Boisgelin belonged to the minor nobility and his family was long established in Provence. Contrary to received tradition there were many such families in France, content to serve their king by service to their native province and unattracted by the pageantry of Versailles. In temperament and in their attitude to those depending upon them they were much closer to the squirearchy of England. One member of the family, it is true, became a cardinal, but he was a Napoleonic creation, and his elevation cannot have been applauded by his royalist relatives.

Louis de Boisgelin seems to have travelled widely in Northern Europe before the Revolution. During the siege of Toulon in 1793 he became a captain in a royalist regiment, the Royal-Louis. The British fleet, which the inhabitants of Toulon had invited into their harbour, was driven out by Napoleon's brilliant bombardment and de Boisgelin, who had been wounded, was evacuated with it. Subsequently de Boisgelin took part in the Corsican campaign, and when that ended he was transported to Britain where he was granted a pension by the government. He did not return to France until 1815.

While in Britain he quartered the country. A dozen or so notebooks, written in his crabbed and minuscule hand, survive in the Bibliothèque Méjanes at Aix-en-Provence. They demonstrate his scientific and literary disposition, his insatiable curiosity and his passion for factual detail. It is obvious that he read English fluently. His notebooks contain a précis of Samuel Johnson's *Tour* and he must have been able to communicate adequately. The year 1797 saw him in Scotland—not, it would seem, for the first time, but it is from that year that we have his fullest account of Edinburgh.

Of the Royal Mile he notes that

> the dirtiest part of the street is that which leads to Holyrood House, the former palace of the Kings of Scotland and which forms the end of the street. Holyrood House has a park which measures about four miles in circumference and its enclosure forms a good defence against creditors. Monsieur the Comte d'Artois was there for that reason, going out only on Sundays and *jours de fête*.

De Boisgelin did not find the palace itself impressive, but he notes that the rooms were spacious, which suggests that he penetrated the interior, and that the part occupied by Monsieur included the apartments of Mary, Queen of Scots, which, he says, contained little of real interest. He mentions sardonically that the blood-stains of Rizzio were still on show, which indicates that someone had explained to him that the floor in question had been raised six feet during Bruce's reconstruction in the seventeenth century.

Loyalist though he was and wounded in the royal cause, de Boisgelin does not seem to have had any personal contact with Artois or his entourage. Perhaps the chasm dividing the courtiers of Versailles and the provincial nobility remained too great even in exile. In other respects de Boisgelin was a fascinated and critical observer of the Edinburgh scene. He was much struck by the puritanical behaviour of the Scots:

> On Sundays and *jours de fête* it is forbidden to play cards or any kind of musical instrument. All social gatherings are strictly forbidden. During my stay in Edinburgh, Lady Campbell, a very fashionable and rich lady, insisted on giving a party on a Sunday. The following Sunday every pulpit resounded with fulminations against such a scandal; the magistrates themselves spoke to Lady Campbell and I am sure that for some time to come there will be no more question of such an assembly to relieve the Sunday monotony. Before the morning service Edinburgh is an absolute desert, literally no-one goes out

> before the first peal of bells. Hardly have the bells begun to ring than a large mass of people, all well dressed, are to be seen moving towards their different chapels, observing a sort of religious silence, and scarcely giving each other more than a passing greeting.

De Boisgelin acknowledges a more positive side to this picture: 'The Scottish peasant is most abstemious. One sees very few Scottish soldiers, hielanders, in the hospitals suffering from venereal disease.' [*maladies suite de débauches honteuses.*] Indeed, of the Scottish character in general he is full of praise.

> The increase of wealth and industry in Scotland . . . is unexampled . . . During the last twenty years the number of Scots who have made a considerable fortune is unbelievable, for the most part in India or in the land forces, less often in the Navy. The love of their native land has impelled the greater part of these Scots to return to live there and to improve the home of their father or the house which they have bought.

He adds that most of the generals on active service in 1795 were Scots. This statement has not been checked and might well be disputed by the Irish.

De Boisgelin concludes his general observations on Scotland with this paragraph:

> The English have in general no conception of the wealth existing in Scotland today. I have spoken several times to people who are supposed to be well instructed about Scotland and I have not met one who could give me any real information about the country. Most of them wished to persuade me not to go there, representing it to me as a barbarous land where there was nothing to be seen save a few interesting views in the mountains.

The 'heather begins at Luton' syndrome, so prevalent today, has a long ancestry.

To return to the City of Edinburgh, the first thing that impressed de Boisgelin was the difference between the old town and the new, which 'presents itself in the most magnificent way'.

He continues

> The contrast between the two towns is indeed striking; the houses on the one side new, neat and of uniform style; on the other old, dirty and ill-constructed,

> some of them having up to twelve or thirteen stories; their windows are very small and the alleys narrow. Taking the bridge one arrives at the old town which [the new road] spans. This road is already very fine and will become even more so when all the houses are re-built—and this is near completion—and when the College is finished, which, given the size of the building, will not be soon even if it is true that the war has held up the work.

Of the Royal Mile, he says that it had kept its original aspect:

> Nothing can be compared to the darkness and filth of the narrow pends leading from the right and left of the street. Fortunately Edinburgh is a very windy city, for it is to be feared that the filth piled up in these alleys and in the very staircases of many of the houses might otherwise give rise to contagious diseases, all the more dangerous since I have never seen humanity so closely packed together.

Few travellers of the period have so assiduously covered the sights of Edinburgh. There is a long description of the Infirmary which receives much criticism: 'The bedding is bad and insufficient, the blankets dirty and not long enough and the beds have no curtains.' 'There is a place for surgical instruments; I found them in poor condition; many were rusty and they were few in number. The dispensary . . . is on a ground floor, not very large and, I fear to say it, not clean.' He does, however, praise the Infirmary as a centre of surgical teaching.

The law courts attracted his attention and his description tallies with that of Lord Cockburn in his *Memorials*. In Parliament Hall 'there were three separate judges each holding his own court, and I cannot conceive how they were able to hear or make themselves heard for four or five hundred people were walking up and down . . . and the noise made by this assembly may well be imagined.'

Parliament Square was *fort petite*, doubtless in comparison with the Place Louis XV, now the Place de la Concorde; the equestrian statue of Charles II no better than middling. He was impressed by the bookshops and admired the new Royal Exchange building, today the City Chambers, but 'on entering the courtyard one is astonished by the irregularity of the buildings which surround it.'

The Castle, of course, was visited and the new barracks holding 800 foot soldiers duly noted. 'From the Castle a wide and delightful view can be obtained.' His highest praise was kept for the Calton Hill. 'The view and the variety of perspective are to be compared with all the similar views which I have seen, not excepting Naples and the lighthouse at Messina.'

He notes the Mound under construction—vehicles are using it already; he visits Leith—the half-hourly omnibus costs sixpence, which, impliedly, he thinks reasonable. Given that sixpence would then buy a substantial meal one is not so sure. He makes a tour of Heriot's Hospital and George Watson's College, the college of 'George Voiston'. The pupils at the latter are 'all sons of merchants and are taught Latin and French . . . They are fed very frugally, meat only three times a week, other days milk and very good white bread.'

On the social side, the Assembly Rooms in George Street are commended, as is St Cecilia's Hall in the old town. At St Cecilia's Hall the elegant interior is contrasted with a poor external appearance:

> There are balls and assemblies to which one may subscribe at a modest price. Foreigners may easily obtain tickets and I was present at several. Though I had been told that they were well attended, I was not impressed, accustomed as I was to those of Bath. Facing the entrance was a table behind which sat the Queen of the Ball in an armchair. There was no Master of Ceremonies here and I observed that the women were not, in general, as well turned out as in London or even Bath.

He is struck by the fact that many of the women were tall and slender: 'Both men and women keep better time than in England.'

> The English *contre-dances* [by which he must mean quadrilles] are danced with the same sobriety as in England, but the moment a Scottish reel, which are the tunes of the country, is struck up everyone is transformed and animated and one might believe oneself carried away among men and women who had been suddenly metamorphosed; the dancing is as lively as it might be in Provence or in Spain when they dance the fandango. The ladies' white cheeks turn to a charming pink and their eyes sparkle. Truly the sudden change operated by the first notes of one of their national airs is not to be imagined.

As has been said, there is no direct evidence that those closest to Artois shared de Boisgelin's lively and inquisitive approach. Nonetheless, living in the Canongate with the brimful life of Edinburgh around them, so vividly described by the observant captain, and with ample time to experience it, one cannot believe that they did not sense its pulsating force. Perhaps, like their compatriots in London, they found it merely 'tiresome and odd'.

CHAPTER 10

Artois returns to the North, 1801

At the beginning of October 1801 Artois wrote from London to Robert Dundas of Arniston, who earlier that year had been made Chief Baron, that is to say, the senior judge of the Exchequer Court, that 'I hasten to announce that with the approval of His Britannic Majesty, I count on returning at once to Edinburgh'. The exact date of Artois's return is not known, but on 1 December Patrick Murray, the King's Remembrancer, is writing to Lord Breadalbane, who was still seeking to recover his rooms in the Palace, informing him that 'His Majesty has been pleased to grant permission to Monsieur to re-occupy the apartments in the Palace formerly possessed by him together with those possessed by Lord Adam Gordon'. For the next two years Edinburgh was, once again, to be Artois's principal place of residence.

In his letter to Chief Baron Dundas Artois expresses his pleasure at the prospect of being at home once more among a nation which had inspired him with so many sentiments of affection, but he is explicitly reticent about his reasons for coming north, and further deduction is impeded by his handwriting, illegible as ever. The biographer of Madame de Lage suggests his only purpose in visiting Scotland after 1798 was to enjoy the shooting available 'on the mountains of Scotland, abounding in game', but the object of his journey north was more fundamental.

The truth is to be found in a memorandum by Louis XVIII and by Artois, dated December 1801, and addressed to the British Government. Despite a careful search in the Public Record Office at Kew, no English version, which diplomatic usage would have required, can be found. The only text available is one in French in the Archives of the Quai d'Orsay. This memorandum must be placed in its context. Artois owed his release from the confines of Holyrood to the immunity provided by the Aliens Act of 1798. This, however was a temporary measure and its successor, the Aliens Act of 1800, only continued the operation of the 1798 Act 'until six months after the conclusion of a general peace'. At the time when Artois was writing to the Chief Baron there were many indications that such a general peace would be concluded. Early in 1801 Napoleon had defeated the Austrians in the battles of Marengo and Hohenlinden and by the Treaty of Luneville had gained control of almost the whole of Western Europe. Only Britain remained at war with him and she, despite her victories in Egypt and at Copenhagen, was in an extremely vulnerable position. Pitt, Grenville and Henry Dundas, the uncrowned king of Scotland, were forced to resign and, under the new government of Addington, negotiations for peace were begun which culminated in the short-lived Peace of Amiens, the Treaty being signed in March 1802.

Accordingly, in the closing months of 1801 Artois and many other *émigrés* were in danger of arrest for debts contracted abroad should peace be declared and should no further legislative action be taken. It was essential for their security that the British Government be persuaded to legislate. Prudence also dictated that Monsieur, who was by far the largest debtor concerned, should apply such pressure as he could from a position of safety. Artois was thus once again ensconced in Holyrood by the time the Memorandum was presented.

The Memorandum opens with a description of the plight of the *émigrés* who had incurred debts abroad and pays tribute to the benevolence of the British Government. Nevertheless

> a state of ill will has come to disturb their haven of rest, as if jealous of their escape from misfortune; cut off from the land of their birth, liable to a capital sentence should they dare to return, they have been persecuted and actions have been raised in England against those who have not had the good luck to find guarantors and whose future is that of endless imprisonment.

The Memorandum then refers to the legislation in force, that is to say the Aliens Act of 1800, which 'was related to the circumstances of the war which is coming to an end' and elaborates at length the reasons, legal and moral, why the existing protection should be extended:

> The peace between England and France brings about no change in the state of those who remain expatriates, whether of necessity or by reason of scruples which do them credit; all alike should be able to count on the protection and benevolence of a government which has manifested its protection of rights long held or of those who by their conduct have acquired such rights.

As regards the position of Louis XVIII and Artois the Memorandum asserts that their debts fall into two categories, public and private:

Public debts may be classified as those which the King and Monsieur contracted in 1792: they were for the cause of equipping those Frenchmen who remained faithful to their duty and for the costs of the campaign which followed on the invitation by the allied powers to the French Princes to join them. It would not be right to allow proceedings for debts of this character, since they were incurred by the princes essentially to satisfy the calls made upon them.

The private debts of Monsieur and the King are those which were personal to them before the Revolution; there are at present absolutely no others; and debts of this kind are to be classified with those of other *émigrés*. The French nation has taken away their patrimony, has over-run their estates, in the same way as those of private citizens. The same principle which should be a defence against the creditors of the *émigrés* applies to those of the French Princes.

Artois concludes this document with an expression of confident expectation that appropriate measures will be taken not only to assure his personal tranquillity but also for the safety of those 'whose attachment to his misfortunes compel them to share his fate'.

In the long run Artois's fears were groundless, but ineluctably they were intensified by the signature of the Treaty of Amiens in March 1802. Thus, there followed a second memorandum which referred to its predecessor and to Article 14 of the Treaty which made the Courts competent to decide '*toutes reclamations*', i.e. any legal claims. Artois comments, 'After that provision is it not to be feared that henceforth grasping creditors will dare to arrest their debtors?'

Monsieur warms to his subject and again refers to the confiscation of goods by the French Republic and to the destruction of title deeds, making it impossible to decide whether claims are justifiable or not. He then adds yet another item to the list of dangers besetting the *émigrés*.

There is proof that '*lettres de change*' or '*billets à ordre*' [types of promissory note] (the only type which in France give an action against the person) are being presented for enforcement subscribed by persons arrested under the regime of Robespierre although bearing a date long before the date of their captivity; these obligations were to be the price of their liberty—an illusory promise! Although the billet might equal almost the total of their fortune, the guillotine was the reward of their credulity. Nevertheless the bearer of the instrument, taking refuge in London from his crimes and evil doing has not blushed to present it to the children or heirs of his lamented victims.

The lamented victims, according to Artois, were thereby threatened with the prospect of proceedings as soon as the protection afforded by the Act of 1798 was removed.

Artois's wishes would appear to have been fulfilled by the Aliens Act of 1802 which 'made perpetual' the immunity conferred by the earlier legislation. Unfortunately for Monsieur and his fellow *émigrés* the Peace of Amiens came to an end in May, 1803. The resumption of hostilities was followed by the Aliens Act of 1803 which repealed the whole of the Act of 1802, including the perpetuity clause. While the new act safeguarded all 'Aliens abiding in the United Kingdom who have quitted their respective Countries by reason of any Revolution or Troubles in France' the Act was only to continue in force 'until three months after the Ratification of the Definitive Treaty of Peace'.

While the war lasted, and it was to continue until 1814, Artois and his compatriots no longer needed to fear that they might be arrested for debts which they had incurred abroad. On the other hand, decades later, there were to be repercussions. These memoranda, however, and the legislation which they generated, provide a more convincing reason than the attractions of the grouse moor for Artois's presence in Scotland until 1803 and they explain why, until the second exile of 1830, there is, with one possible exception, no recorded trace of his having visited Scotland after 1803.

CHAPTER 11

Behind the Scenes in 1802

On the surface the year 1802 seems to have passed uneventfully enough, though, as will appear, much was going on behind the scenes. Madame de Lage was in Edinburgh for three months which must have given great pleasure to the increasingly consumptive Louise de Polastron. The Treaty of Amiens had been signed in March. Bonaparte was in course of making himself consul for life and soon, in the backlash of an abortive royalist plot which appears to have been the gossip of the drawing-rooms of Edinburgh, was to crown himself Emperor.

Except for the most ardent royalist—and those surrounding Artois were the most ardent—the Peace of Amiens was an opportunity for many *émigrés* to accept the new order and return to France. It is an over-simplification to describe Napoleon as an outrageous snob, but there is no doubt that for him the Almanach de Gotha had an irresistible appeal. With the crown of Empire already within his sights he was determined to provide himself with a court. He could, and indeed did, create his own aristocracy but, as in other fields, there was no substitute for the genuine article. If necessary he was very ready to import it and to that end grant amnesty to such *émigrés* as returned.

Even so devoted a royalist as Madame de Lage was seduced by the prospect of returning to her native land, and it is ironical that after all her suffering in the cause of the monarchy her destination on quitting Edinburgh in August 1802 should be none other than Paris. To be fair to her and to anticipate events, her devotion to the Comte d'Artois re-asserted itself after the July Revolution of 1830. She then left France for ever and died in exile at Baden in 1842 at the age of 78.

The amnesty offered by Napoleon was not well received in all quarters. Vaudreuil, writing from Edinburgh on 6 May 1802, was angry indeed:

> Have you ever seen anything to equal or harsher or more humiliating than this amnesty? That man seeks to degrade all who are opposed to him, royalty, religion and loyal subjects. Do you see me of their number? . . . at least you will not have to blush for my apostasy.

The year 1802 saw the promulgation of Napoleon's Concordat with the Papacy. Pious VII, 'a simple and pious monk with little knowledge of the world', as Professor Cobban describes him, had recognised the pre-eminence of the French state in all matters ecclesiastical, the alienation of church lands and the payment by the state of all church stipends. From henceforth, no priest could perform his office, no papal bull could be published without the authority of the state. This news greatly disturbed Monsieur in the Presbyterian fastness of Edinburgh:

> I have never seen him so profoundly moved as he has been this last fortnight and I am in no state to console him. For to me the outlook is even blacker than for him. When the Head of the Church abandons the interest of religion and the cause of kings who is there on whom one can rely?

So wrote Vaudreuil to his mother on 17 April 1802.

Despite these setbacks Monsieur felt sufficiently sure of his position to travel widely in Scotland and to accept hospitality wherever it was offered. In August he was at Gordon Castle, the seat of the notorious rake Alexander, fourth Duke of Gordon, whose infidelities were only matched by those of his wife, the Duchess Jane, the eponymous founder of the Gordon Highlanders. The Duke of Atholl entertained Artois at Blair and, as always, there were the Buccleuchs at Dalkeith, where, after having been received on one occasion by the Duchess, Artois is reported as saying that it was as if she was some mighty sovereign and he an insignificant foreigner.

The summer of 1802 in Scotland provided the occasion for a family gathering. In August the Duc de Berry arrived at Leith aboard an Excise ship, *The Prince of Wales*, and was present at the election of Scotland's representative peers in the Palace of Holyroodhouse like Artois six years before. He also took part in what was described as an 'elegant entertainment' at the Tontine Tavern and a 'brilliant assembly at the Rooms in George Street', rooms in daily use today. Scotland also witnessed a surprisingly amicable royal reconciliation between Artois and Berry, on the one hand, and, on the other, an Orleans prince, the Duc de Monpensier, a son of the Duc d'Orleans, the future King Louis-Phillipe who was to de-throne Artois in 1830, and a grandson of 'Philippe-Egalité', the regicide, who had voted for the death of Louis XVI.

We are fortunate in getting an intimate picture of Artois at this period. Lady Louisa Stuart, the youngest daughter of the Earl of Bute and a grand-daughter of the eccentric Lady Mary Wortley Montague, was one of the most talented and witty correspondents of her day. From the family estates at Luton Hoo, Wharncliffe in Yorkshire, and during frequent visits to London, Bath and the greater houses of Scotland, she had the opportunity of seeing all that happened and of recording it with charm and perspicacity. From Bothwell Castle, from which she had attended the Hamilton races, she writes on 22 October 1802:

> Even in my young days, I am sure that I never went to four balls in one week before. They were not four running, for we lay by on Wednesday night, and went Monday, Tuesday, Thursday and Friday, but to make amends we were at the course on Wednesday morning and on Saturday the Duc de Berri came before we were out of bed to spend the day. He had returned to Hamilton Palace for the races when Monsieur went back to Edinburgh.

Lady Louisa continues:

> You may think yourself well off if I do not pester you with French words and phrases. Talking and hearing nothing else for four whole days has left nothing else in my head. Monsieur brought with him his youngest son, the Duc de Berri, and three gentlemen, the Chevalier de Puységur, a very lively entertaining man; the Baron de Roll, an honest Swiss, whom I have seen at Lord Macartney's and often at different places in London . . . Monsieur himself is a very handsome healthy-looking man, remarkably well made, above the middle size and stout. He looks much younger than his age (45) and has a splendid open countenance but his mouth does not shut, the upper lip being too short. For his air and manner, it is as I will not say gentleman-like only, but noble and prince-like, as you can imagine, with that sort of high and dignified good breeding, that gracious civility to everybody (with, at the same time, the greatest ease), you would expect from a prince bred in the politest court in Europe.

Lady Louisa compares Artois with the Prince of Wales:

> He has not so fine an air and is not nearly so handsome as *our* Prince, but I fancy excels him in conversation, because he is easy and pleasant without mimicry or determination to laugh at something, in short, like any other agreeable man; but there is so great a resemblance of manner to the Prince, and also to the P.'s father, tho' the latter, dear good man, is as you know *gauche* and awkward and Monsieur the reverse, that I should have said anywhere, 'Why that man looks like something royal'.

Lady Louisa Stuart is, however, less enthusiastic about the Duc de Berry.

> As for his son, nobody would find him out for a prince or a gentleman, and less for a soldier than either, tho', poor youth! he has passed his life in hard warfare, having always served with the Armée de Condé, and, they say, behaved extremely well. But his appearance is against him; he is little, thick, stumpy and slouching, with a very ugly brown face that might be fifty years old and a sullen down look yet certainly does not seem to want sense or observation. If his mother were like him in person it may account for some of poor Monsieur's past irregularities, for she must have been very disgusting to a gay young prince whom all the pretty women in France are desirous to attract, very different from our poor little friend Madame de Can who was his first flame.

'Madame de Can' is no doubt Madame de Canillac, Artois's companion at the encounter with the Duchesse de Bourbon at the Shrove Tuesday ball of 1778 and, for once, Lady Louisa Stuart is a little naive. Madame de Canillac was far from being Artois's 'first flame.'

The social manners and graces, or rather the lack of them, of the Scots male do not escape Lady Louisa's sharp eye and ear:

> By the bye, this gave me an opportunity of observing that men can be just as illiberal and narrow-minded as women, even very ignorant and frivolous women, for no misses could have been more disposed to quiz some poor person, their superior in sense and character, for not being exactly dressed in the fashion of the day than our gentlemen were these Frenchmen, for not shooting exactly in the English manner, as if it were the most contemptible thing in the world and the business itself was of importance instead of a diversion.

The same occasion is also described by Lady Louisa's cousin, Lady Lothian, in a letter to her mother, the Duchess of Buccleuch:

> Oct. 1802
>
> M. de Puységur was beyond himself entertaining both at that first dinner and yesterday's, but particularly yesterday . . . I have really these two days been quite knocked up at night with the laughing of the day.

The examples which she gives, however, do not wear well and one will suffice:

> At dinner again we sat as usual, and as usual there was a good deal of entertaining conversation. 'Monsieur' declared that he should be happy to set out immediately for China, so much does he like the sea. Monsieur Puységur,

who hates it as much, said, '*Eh bien, allons-y, Monsieur, on dit que l'empereur est fort poli*'. The idea of the Emperor of China being polite, is good, I think.

Nonetheless, the witticisms of M. de Puységur had a durable quality. Twenty years later Lady Louisa Stuart recalls, 'Monsieur de Puységur when in Edinburgh (with Monsieur) proposed to buy a sentry-box "Pour avoir un lieu à soi" [to have a place of one's own]—a droll thought, but it expresses a great deal to the mind of an Englishman.'

Of greater interest is Lady Lothian's account of de Puységur in a more serious vein, away from the presence of Artois and relieved of his role as Court jester:

> . . . he told us a great deal about the excessive *tristesse* of their society, chiefly to him since the Vaudreuils and the Duc de Maillé went away, as they had been *de sa société* before from choice; but that the set at present are very good and worthy people, but not all these he should choose for his companions or constant friends. He then launched out in praise of 'Monsieur', who he said, he believed was '*le meilleur caractère que le ciel eut jamais formé*, so constantly aimiable and cheerful and (*aussi peu exigeant et craignant de nous gêner, que s'il était un particulier*) [so little demanding and fearful of disturbing us, as if he were a private citizen] and as satisfied from the first with every privation as if he had never known better.'

De Puységur had a revealing comment to make on Louise de Polastron, according to Lady Lothian, 'He said that Madame de Polastron was *triste*, always *malade* and *aigrie* [embittered]: one would think, seeing [Artois] exert himself so much, if she is so much attached to him, would make her long to do so too.'

On the other hand he was unexpectedly tolerant of those who had been close to Artois but who had decided to return to France. One such had been the Duc de Maillé, constantly of the company at Holyrood. According to Lady Lothian, de Puységur had said, 'how cruel it was to judge hastily of those emigrants who were returned, and particularly the Duc de Maillé, who, if he has now to leave France, would make his children perfect beggars; as for himself, he said he could speak impartially on the subject as he has nothing at all to expect if he were to return.'

A social footnote, comes from Lady Louisa, written later that same year:

> I am very much tired of plough-boys and postillions, and cannot regret that Bonaparte, who seems to be the most magnificent as well as the most absolute

> Prince since Louis Quatorze, insists upon full dress and swords in his presence, for I hope that it must change the fashion, but do not betray my old-fashioned ideas to the young ladies. Poor Monsieur surprised those here by lamenting the disuse of powder and sweet pomatum, which he said used to salute one's nose on entering a publick place, whereas the heads, to be sure, are not in general odiferous; the younger part of us were very much disturbed that he *could* wish to see people such *quizzes*, and are very confident that if hoops, bags and powder come again into fashion, *nothing should ever make them submit* to wear anything so preposterous. I daresay you will say the same.

Despite the superficial banter, despite the hospitality of the Scottish nobility, 1802 was not a happy year for Artois and his little court. The restoration of the monarchy seemed as far away as ever. 'Bonaparte is the conqueror; he lays down the law to those he has vanquished, and if among them there are some with good intentions they are firmly of the view that they will not renew hostilities for our cause alone', wrote Vaudreuil to Louis XVIII. For the *émigrés* money affairs predominated. For Vaudreuil in particular it was a year of acute anxiety. His letters from Edinburgh, or after his departure, from London are full of the absence of revenue from San Domingo, then a target of a Bonapartist expedition under General Leclerc.

CHAPTER 12

A Napoleonic Spy in Edinburgh: The King goes back to London, 1803

While news of France was eagerly sought in Scotland the reverse was also true. The traffic was two-way. Napoleon had become alarmed at rumours of royalist plotting in Edinburgh. On 13 June 1802 Talleyrand, who, with acrobatic skill, had become French Foreign Minister, wrote to General Andréossy, the ambassador in London of the Consulate during the Peace of Amiens, instructing him to send a man to Edinburgh to report on the activities of Monsieur and his friends. Andréossy replied that he had found a man 'who knew all about the emigration'. We shall probably never know the identity of the spy nor how he achieved an entrée to Artois's circle, but he addresses the ambassador in an easy and self-assured manner. Copies of his reports to Andréossy are to be found, neatly filed, in the archives of the Quai d'Orsay. To see and to read them is to share the surprise of the citizens of Edinburgh had they known that there was a chiel among them taking notes for the all-seeing eyes of Talleyrand. The first report is dated 20 January 1803 and deserves to be quoted almost in full:

> It is already a fortnight since I arrived but I have difficulty in remembering it. Thanks to the introductions which my friend has given me I am on the road to being of some use to you, at least I hope so, for I have already seen certain people who can, if they have sufficient good-will, give me the information which you seek. But you must realise that there is a considerable gap between a formal visit and frank and friendly discussion. It may therefore take me some time before you are satisfied with this correspondence.
>
> I do not find more among my fugitive compatriots than hot-headed ideas of violence. Would you believe it but someone is still busying himself with a scheme of kidnapping like that of Clément de Riz? [This was a reference to a senator who had been kidnapped by royalist forces] Should the kidnapping, if it could be achieved, be one of the family of the First Consul, or at least some senior official of the state? How would one escape from the pursuit of the police or convey the prisoner to some safe hiding place? . . . This plot has been devised *chez* Georges who resides some miles from London in order to be less

conspicuous and at whose house meet the numerous conspirators. It is said that the person whose idea this is and to whom is confided the principal part in carrying out the scheme is an adventurer who calls himself the Marquis de la Chapelle and who lives near Portman Square.

The 'Georges' mentioned was Georges Cadoudal, the leader of the resistance in the Vendée whom we have already met. He had been involved in a royalist plan of Christmas Eve 1800 to blow up Napoleon on his way to the opera—'the affair of the rue Niçaise'. The explosion caused enormous carnage but came too late to injure Bonaparte. Napoleon, however, put the incident to good use. Although he knew who was behind the plot he chose instead to accuse his Jacobin opponents and arranged for 129 of the most vociferous to be transported to Cayenne and the Seychelles. This deflected attention from the true conspirators and Georges Cadoudal succeeded in escaping to England.

Careless talk in Edinburgh must have been abundant for Andréossy's spy to have learnt so much in a fortnight. It also suggests that he must have had impeccably royalist credentials. Another plot was indeed being prepared although it seems that later the object became assassination rather than kidnapping. In the event, this plot also failed. Cadoudal was arrested and executed, and, as will be recounted, a young group of Artois's closest associates were captured and condemned to death. This abortive attempt was the last direct involvement by the monarchy on the mainland of Europe until the Restoration of 1814.

It is apparent, too, from this report that the presence of Louise de Polastron still caused murmurings among the bourgeoisie of Edinburgh:

I can tell you yet but little about the Princes. Their residence in this town is the pride of the nobility. Everyone concerns themselves with their fate and I have yet to meet someone who does not fulminate against the French Government but I have not yet seen enough to be sure that this is the general attitude. What I can say positively is that it is regarded with considerable disapproval that the Prince has never called his wife to his side and that he houses his mistress in a small but separate house not more than ten paces from the Palace.

There was no denying, however, Monsieur's general popularity. In his next letter, dated 11 March, Andréossy's agent writes:

The Comte d'Artois went to the theatre last Saturday to see the new company of actors. As soon as he appeared in his box loud applause broke out in every corner. Those who were in the boxes stood up to show their respect. The Prince greeted them graciously and the applause was redoubled. You can judge from this fact the truth of my observation as regards public opinion or, more exactly, as regards the opinion of the nobility.

There were some exceptions even among the nobility. One such was the eccentric Earl of Buchan of whom it was reported by Andréossy's spy that he 'never let an occasion pass when he can disapprove of the Prince and the honour accorded to him'. Indeed, Lord Buchan nearly caused a major embarrassment at the Queen's Ball, held in the Assembly rooms in George Street. On this occasion,

> the Captain of the Guard went before the Prince to the accompaniment of the orchestra and, when the Prince entered the hall, everyone was ordered to stand back and let him pass. At all this fuss Lord Buchan called out 'Who is that? Is the King of the shoe-makers coming?' A burst of laughter was heard and some of the spectators gave the most marked signs of approval, not so much because of the coarseness of the remark but more because it served as a reminder of the equality reigning among the notable company attending the Assembly. Lord Buchan, whose wife, I believe, was one of the presidents of the ball, then approached the officer and asked whether he had the orders of the King to behave in such a manner. Lord Buchan then took his place in the passage leading to the room where the Prince and his suite had deployed themselves. 'What,' said someone to him, 'are you going to join the Court?' 'Yes, indeed,' he said, roaring with laughter, 'I feel more at ease with the Court because there is never any crowd'. The Duc de Berry, who heard this conversation, could scarcely restrain himself but the Prince remained wholly silent.

In the end Artois's invariable good manners prevailed and all was well.

> For the rest of the evening, when the first quarter of an hour of formality was over, the Comte d'Artois was full of gaiety, coming and going with the greatest amiability, speaking to everyone, paying civilities to all and sundry and laughing a lot. His good humour was such that he scandalised some stiff Britons. 'What do you think of the Comte?' said one of them to my friend Sir W—— N——, [presumably Sir William Nairne, Lord Dunsinane, the Scottish judge] 'you would think that he was at home and we were *émigrés*.'

The author of the letter also observes that, 'The Prince wore at this ball a plain blue coat without decorations. Last year he had arrived with all the decorations and orders imaginable. Some of the Lords were displeased at this sacrifice as much of their vanity as his own.'

We also learn a little of the protocol in force at this time:

> The Comte d'Artois had wished to hold levees as he did during his first period of residence in the city. Lord Buchan declaimed with force throughout society against this ridiculous pretension and the levees have not taken place.

This is corrected in a later report. There had in fact been levees for a month or so but they were abandoned as a result of Lord Buchan's protests. The report continues,

> The Prince sometimes goes for walks on the pavements of the New Town but he is always accompanied by a dozen courtiers, among whom is always to be found the Captain of the Guard and the *Grand-Ecuyer* etc. At the palace he is accorded a guard of honour; sentries are always on duty before the main entry.

The guard was, in all likelihood, furnished by the garrison at Edinburgh Castle, so the Captain of the Guard would have been a British officer. Who among the French laid claim to the imposing title of *Grand Ecuyer* is not stated, but was almost certainly the Marquis de Rivière, aide-de camp to Artois from the beginning of the emigration, and sometimes referred to as *écuyer*.

By the end of March 1803 Artois's stay in Edinburgh was coming to an end. Bonaparte's refusal to honour either the letter or the spirit of the Treaty of Amiens made it plain that hostilities would have to be resumed. There were many in London who doubted the wisdom of the treaty in the first place and this view was shared abroad. Prussia and Austria disliked the territorial arrangements in Germany, and as a family the Hapsburgs resented the Protestant weighting which the treaty had imposed upon the Electoral College of the Holy Roman Empire. Andréossy's spy accordingly reports on the movements of naval vessels and the activities of the press gang on the east coast of Scotland—three hundred had been forced aboard in Leith alone.

'At Holyrood they are ardently wishing for war to come and no-one hides the hope that it will be declared,' wrote the spy on 29 March, adding that 'The Duc de Berry is about to leave for London. The secretary of the Comte d'Artois, M. de Belleville, is also there at this moment, and I do not doubt that his purpose is to make the arrangements necessary for the Princes' residence in that capital.'

Thinking, perhaps, of himself, Andréossy's man adds,

> This state of uncertainty bears hardly upon Frenchmen who are attached to their motherland. In a little while it will be impossible for them to appear in

the streets without being insulted, and they will not have more ardent persecutors than their compatriots who have here passed the greater part of the revolution. These latter everywhere declare that they alone should have the privilege of remaining in England and to obtain that right one should have to prove in all due form that one was an *émigré*.

On 9 April the spy reports:

Eight days ago the Duc de Berry sent off his baggage to London and he proposes to leave himself in a week's time. He will be accompanied by the Duc d'Harcourt and by M. de Belleville . . . The former will go from London to France: I do not know whether he has taken the necessary legal steps to make the journey in safety, but if he leaves secretly his movements must be watched. The Duc d'Harcourt is one of the most intimate associates of the Prince, especially since the Baron de Roll left this country to intrigue in London concerning the affairs of Switzerland.

The reference to the Duc d'Harcourt is interesting, since he had for a long time been the accredited agent of Louis XVIII in London, and at one time dealings between Artois and d'Harcourt had been at arm's length.

The letter, however, conveys more important news, although its importance could not have been appreciated at the time by either the sender or the recipient—the news of the death on 30 March of Agläe de Polignac, Duchesse de Guiche, the intimate of Louise de Polastron at school at the Abbaye de Panthémont and who had shared her presentation at the court of Versailles:

Sadness reigns in the Palace of Holyroodhouse. The Comtesse [sic] de Guiche died last Wednesday. Her body has been put in a lead coffin and laid in a vault until the family can once again enter France and arrange to have it moved there. The event has interrupted the innocent pleasures of the dramatic performances which the French *émigrés* often give among themselves.

No contemporary account has been traced of the death of Agläe de Guiche. It appears, however, from a family history, that she had been staying in an Edinburgh inn when the clothes of her twelve-year old daughter were set alight by the fire in a room which they were occupying. In an attempt to extinguish the blaze Madame de Guiche was badly burnt and both she and her daughter died shortly afterwards. Surprisingly enough this macabre episode was not reported by the Scottish papers nor by the Comtesse de Boigne whose taste for gruesome detail was well developed.

Madame de Boigne, however, explains the significance of the death for the history of France. She mentions Agläe de Guiche's 'serious attachment' to the Marquis de Rivière and her fruitless and bizarre mission at the instance of Artois to seek a compromise with Napoleon. She succeeded in taking tea with Josephine but was otherwise politely shown the door. According to Madame de Boigne, Agläe de Guiche returned to London from this assignment with her 'health greatly shattered' and Monsieur de Rivière 'hastened to her side'. In fact, since Rivière was in Edinburgh it was she who was hastening to be by his side. Be that as it may, it was the Abbé Latil, the chaplain 'without pretensions', who dominated the scene. According to Madame de Boigne,

> he had secured the confidence of the duchess and dominated her entirely. Monsieur de Rivière was denied entrance except to take part in the conversion which had been wrought on the spirit of the invalid. He followed all her wishes and renounced all that might distress her and became the first to adopt the puerile and petty life of devotion which became the hall-mark of the little Court of Monsieur le comte d'Artois.

The death of her old and much loved friend and the manner in which she had been brought to renouce Rivière had a marked effect on Louise de Polastron. According to the spy's reports, Louise by now was appearing little in public and obviously was failing fast. She, too, 'entrusted her heart and conscience to the Abbé Latil,' says Madame de Boigne. This conversion was, for the time being, kept secret from Artois who 'while regretting the Duchesse de Guiche, would mock the mummeries,' [as he put it] 'which had accompanied her death and the paternosters of Rivière.' The death of Louise, the following year in London, was to follow a similar pattern, and, under similar pressure from Latil, Artois's outlook was to undergo a fundamental change. The extreme clericalism which dominated his reign as Charles X can be traced to Holyrood and to the death-bed metamorphosis of the Duchesse de Guiche.

Rivière for his part had need of the Christian fortitude learnt of the Abbé Latil. His career is another story, but he survived to become the Duc de Rivière and ambassador of Charles X to the Sublime Porte. The year after Aglaé's death, however, he was arrested in Paris as one of the conspirators concerned in the plot on Napoleon's life so well forecast by Andréossy's agent. He was condemned to death, then reprieved, and spent many years in prison.

The children of the Comte d'Artois. Left to right, the Duc de Berry, a daughter, ob. 1776, and the Duc d'Angoulême, Possibly by Anne-Rosalie Filleul (*Private collection, Edinburgh*).

'Le Chiffre d'Amour'. Engraving after Fragonard by De Launay.

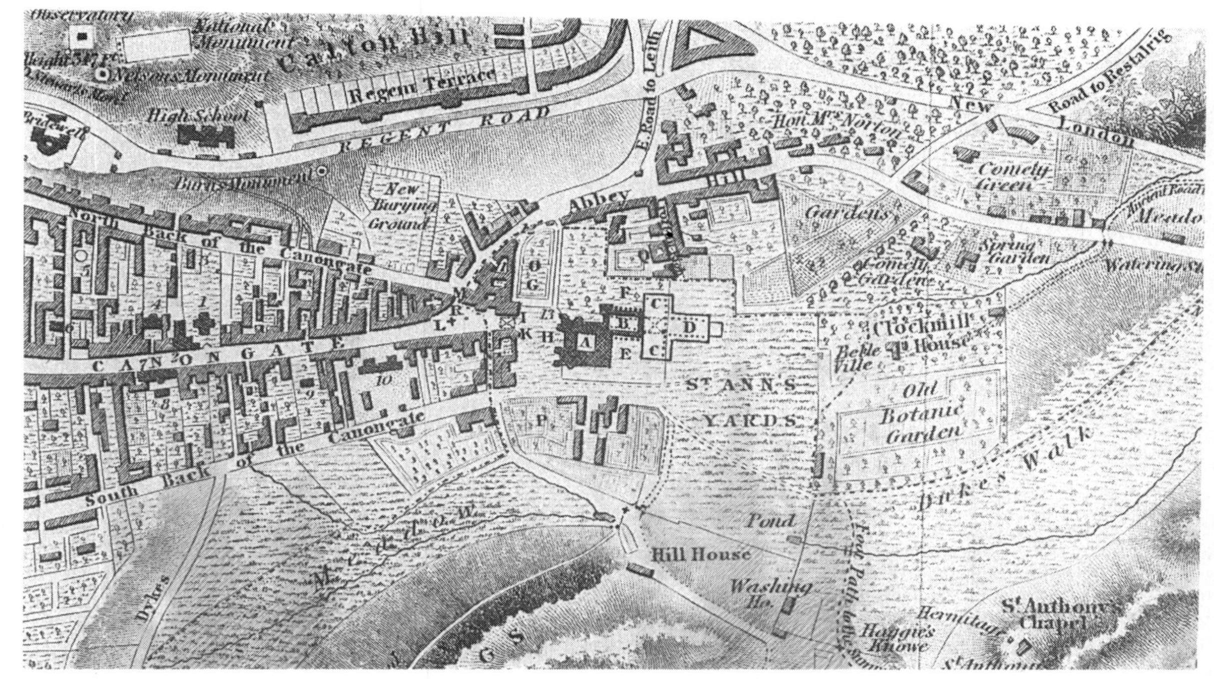

Abbey, sanctuary and environs of Holyrood, 1839 (From *Historical Guide to the Abbey and Palace of Holyrood*, by Henry Courtnoy, Edinburgh, 1838).

Le Comte de Vaudreuil in 1758. François-Hubert Drouais (*Courtesy National Gallery, London*).

Lord Adam Gordon. Henri-Pierre Danloux (*Courtesy Scottish National Portrait Gallery*).

The Comte d'Artois. Henri-Pierre Danloux (*In the collection of the Duke of Buccleuch and Queensberry KT*).

Charles Philippe de France. Engraving after Danloux by Audinet, 1799 (*Courtesy Scottish National Portrait Gallery*).

Louis Antoine, Duc d'Angoulême. Henri-Pierre Danloux (*In the collection of the Duke of Buccleuch and Queensberry KT*).

The third Duke and Duchess of Buccleuch and their family. Henri-Pierre Danloux (*In the collection of Lord Home of the Hirsel KT*).

Louise d'Esparbès, Comtesse de Polastron. Louise Chaceré de Beaurepaire (*whereabouts unknown; after a 1908 illustration*).

Lord Adam Gordon and the Comte d'Artois in 1796. Etching by John Kay (*Courtesy Scottish National Portrait Gallery*).

'The Great and the Small are there.' The Duc d'Angoulême and Major-General Roger Aytoun of Inchdairney. Etching by John Kay (*Courtesy Scottish National Portrait Gallery*).

Holyrood Palace. Colour lithograph by S.D. Swa-breck, 1838 (*Courtesy Edinburgh City Libraries*).

Charles X, King of France, by Sir Thomas Lawrence (*The Royal Collection© Her Majesty The Queen*).

Charles X with Henri, Duc de Bordeaux and the Princesse Louise, 1831. Silhouette by Augustin Edouart (*Private collection, Edinburgh*).

The death of the Duchesse de Guiche was the occasion of much activity in the Abbey Church and the royal vault was rapidly refurbished. The sum of £16 was spent on a new vault door and railings. Instructions were given for the keys to be handed to M. Belleville and to 'Mr. Buchan, Painter', who was to whitewash the vault and 'to have black paint for the painting the church door and the vault door and white for putting dotts thereon'. The exchequer records laconically note:

> The Bones of King James 5th of Scotland, of his Queen and of Henry Lord Darnley, the husband of Queen Mary and of others who were interred in the vault, all of which had for many years been exhibited to the public, were collected and put into a box by command of the Lord Chief Baron. The box was deposited in the vault.

There it remains today.

This did not meet with universal approval. The woman 'beadle' at Holyrood is reported thus by Charles Kirkpatrick Sharp:

> O gentlemen, if ye had cam here a while syne, I cud hae showed ye muckle mair in this place—King James the fifth's shuther and Lord Darnley's thie banes and a guid bit o' the Earl of Buchan's back—but there came a French hizzie that deid here—sae first they pat her in lead coffin and than in a wooden ane, and set her on four stoops and closed up the door—they say she's to gang back to France when the King gets there again—but I think she's still till the Day o' Joodgement.

'This,' said Sharp, 'in a very peevish tone'. Not quite until the Day of Judgement, but long enough. Only in October 1825 did the private secretary to the Duc de Gramond, as the Duc de Guiche had become, present his warrant to the Lord Provost and Magistrates of the City of Edinburgh to receive the remains of the duchess so that they might be transported to Bayonne for interment in the family sepulchre of the Gramonts at Bidache in the Basses Pyrenées.

The exact date of Artois's second departure for London is not recorded, but on 23 April 1803 he was at the Prince de Condé's house at Wanstead where the Bourbon Princes signed a declaration of loyalty to Louis XVIII and affirmed their support for his refusal to surrender his claim to the throne of France whatever consideration might be offered.

Thus the work of Andréossy's spy came to an end. Who was he?

One candidate is the maverick Comte de Montlosier. At first a moderate supporter of the Revolution, he escaped to London where he was the editor of one of the principal *émigré* newspapers, *Le Courrier de Londres*. Turning again, he took exception to the rigid attitudes of many of his fellow Frenchmen whom he there encountered. Even before the Peace of Amiens was signed he had obtained permission to return to France—he had become an admirer of Napoleon—but, characteristically, his public line as the editor of a Paris journal was too independent for the taste of the First Consul. Nonetheless he still remained in favour, since he was taken on the strength of the Ministry of Exterior Relations with an annual salary of 6,000 francs, for, as it was delicately put, 'incidental expenses and exceptional work'. There is no trace of his having been in Britain during the spring of 1803 but equally nothing against it. Why should he not, with his long stay in London, revisit his former friends during the Peace of Amiens, fortified by his newly re-acquired rights as a French citizen and under the protection of Napoleon's ambassador in London?

Another, but remoter possibility, is one Antoine Jeudy Dugour, who in August 1803 had, in fact, been arrested in Dundee as a French spy but who was later released on the reluctant advice of the Lord Advocate, Charles Hope, since interrogation by the Sheriff-depute at Dundee had disclosed nothing incriminating. While at the time of his arrest Dugour held the unpretentious post of schoolmaster in the employment of the Magistrates of Dundee, (salary £25 per year plus half a guinea per pupil), he seems to have been a person of great presence and charm and had among his character references a substantial number of the good and great of Edinburgh who could have assured his entry to polite circles. Equally significantly the same list contained some more suspect names: Montlosier again, Sir John Macpherson, a former Governor-General of Bengal, whose successor described his tenure as a 'system of dirtiest jobbery', but of whom it was said, in the *Dictionary of National Biography*, that 'his tall figure, handsome face and courtly manners made him a great favourite in society; and his wide knowledge and linguistic talents won him the respect of scholars'; and, not least, the eccentric Earl of Buchan. Dugour, incidentally, had a remarkable subsequent history, becoming, in 1812, Director of the University of St Petersburg.

Some day, perhaps, some archival scholar will stumble upon the truth, but, whoever he was, by April 1803 the spy's duties were over. Artois was back in London, once more at 46 Baker Street, while Louise de Polastron, in terminal decline, resided nearby in Thayer Street. Louise was never to see Edinburgh again; and there is only one sighting of Monsieur in Edinburgh during the next twenty-seven years.

CHAPTER 13

The Death of Louise and the Renunciation of Holyroodhouse

Even if the scene shifts to London after April 1803 there are two episodes so closely connected to events in Edinburgh that they merit description. They are, moreover, of importance in any assessment of Artois's character and outlook during the three decades of his life which remained, including his disastrous years as the last King of France and Navarre.

The first was the outcome of the conspiracy described by Andréossy's spy in his first report. In spite of the disapproval of Louis XVIII, those close to Artois remained determined to capture and, if need be, to murder Napoleon. The moving spirit, far-fetched though it may seem, was the stolid Swiss, the Baron de Roll. From the immediate entourage of Holyrood came three allied to the late Duchesse de Guiche, her two brothers, Armand and Jules de Polignac and her *amant* Charles-Francois de Rivière. Also involved were the former Republican general, Pichegru, and, of course, the intrepid Georges Cadoudal. The plan was simple enough in its outline. Bonaparte's coach was to be stopped somewhere between Paris and Malmaison. Napoleon was then to be captured alive and spirited to England. Assassination was to be the last resort.

The first group of conspirators left England in the autumn of 1803 with Cadoudal as their leader. Despite the fact that security in London was even worse than in Edinburgh they were able to land unnoticed at Biville on the Cherbourg peninsula, across the narrows from Jersey. They scaled the cliffs by rope ladders and then, by a series of night journeys, made their way to Paris. There, for the next five months they made contact with potential sympathisers and achieved some success. In particular the indecisive Moreau who had succeeded Pichegru as the Republican commander of the Rhine army in 1793 was persuaded to throw in his lot with the conspirators. One element alone was lacking. It was essential in Cadoudal's view, and he was plainly right, that a Prince of the House of Bourbon should be secreted in Paris to assume control as Lieutenant-General in the name of Louis XVIII once the coup had been announced.

That prince should have been Artois. Once more the cliffs of Biville were the point of disembarkation. Tradition has it that as Georges Cadoudal saw Armand de Polignac emerging from the darkness he called, 'Is the Prince with you?' On receiving a negative answer Georges broke down and, echoing the words of Charette on the Vendée shore eight years before, said aloud, 'We are lost.'

Nevertheless, preparations continued and in January 1804 others arrived at the cliff-top rendezvous, including Jules de Polignac and General Pichegru himself.

The story of their betrayal and capture is the inevitable mixture of venality and courage, rashness and double-dealing. By the end of March all the conspirators were dead or under lock and key. Pichegru was mysteriously strangled while being taken in a covered cart to the Temple. Moreau and Cadoudal were executed and with the death of the latter all active royalist opposition to Napoleon came to an end. Armand and Jules de Polignac were condemned to death as was the Marquis de Rivière. All three were ultimately reprieved but endured long prison sentences in conditions of great hardship. The devotion of these men to Artois was as great as it was misplaced. Indeed, at the moment of his arrest in Paris, Rivière was wearing a portrait of Monsieur, inscribed in his hand, 'Keep yourself safe for the sake of your friends and the struggle against our common enemies.' The date and place of the gift was October 1796 at Holyroodhouse.

Artois's sorrow at the loss of so many of those closest to him is evident in the letters of the period. His sense of debt and obligation, which he never lost, explains the confidence which he placed, often erroneously, upon Jules de Polignac and Charles-Francois de Rivière during his reign.

From a royalist view it may even be said that the aborted plot was counter-productive. The news of the attempted abduction of Napoleon swung popular feeling to his side and made it impossible for another plot to succeed. In its turn, the increasingly impregnable position of Napoleon induced many more *émigrés* to obtain removal of their names from the list of those proscribed and to seek their fortune under the Empire.

Meanwhile in London the diminished inner circle around Artois remained faithful and otherwise occupied. While Cadoudal and his fellow plotters waited in vain for the arrival of Monsieur on the coast of Normandy the latter's main concern was the failing health of Louise de Polastron.

Artois had at first refused to recognise that anything was wrong. At last, Madame de Gontaut insisted upon consulting Sir Henry Halford, physician to the Prince Regent. He at once diagnosed tuberculosis and prescribed the treatment of the day, the steamy atmosphere of fresh dung. The last days of Louise were accordingly spent in the country village of Brompton Grove, (now, so Margery Weiner tells us, Ovington Square in Kensington), in a room fitted up for her above a stable. Louise, realising that death was near and moved by the example of Agläe de Guiche, gave her soul into the hands of the same little priest, with his 'pale face, rounded belly and pointed nose', to quote a contemporary, the Abbé Latil.

The Abbé's technique with Artois was the same as he had adopted with de Rivière. Confession made and absolution given, Artois was banned from the presence of Louise until the moment when she was *in articulo mortis*, an instruction which a more tolerant age might regard as an unnecessarily cruel precondition to ultimate salvation. During her last weeks Louise was strengthened by the companionship of the faithful Madame de Lage, 'Blimonette', who had made an appalling journey of six weeks across Europe in bitter winter to be with her childhood friend. On 27 March 1804 Louise de Polastron died, aged only 39, having in a moving final interview with Artois made him swear that he would thenceforth belong only to God.

The death of Louise and its effect upon Artois belong to a wider history; indeed, they are crucial to any understanding of the conflicts preceding the July Revolution of 1830. Through Louise, Artois was to be totally subject to Latil for the rest of his life. Cardinal Latil would crown him at Rheims and administer the last unction in distant Slovenia. Through Latil he was exposed to the more reactionary forces of the Catholic church. At first in pious memory of Louise but later because these forces struck a response in his nature, Artois found consummation in the teachings of Latil but a consummation which made him unable to appreciate the needs of France in the years following the Restoration. More immediately apparent was the change in Artois's personality after the death of Louise. The dignity remained but from that time on he became withdrawn and solemn. With Louise's death vanished the gaiety, superficial and unintellectual perhaps, but gaiety all the same, with which they had together overcome so much.

Among the Dundas papers at Arniston is a letter from Vaudreuil to the Chief Baron which reflects the mood of this unhappy time. It is dated 16 March 1804:

> Pity us, my lord, in this moment of disaster. The arrest of Moreau and Pichegru has dashed all our hopes and we shudder at the bitter and inevitable loss of two

> great men. As Frenchmen we more than ever blush at the subjection and knavery of a people who show no signs of sparing two generals [Pichegru and Moreau] who by their victories have made the power of France so formidable and have so extended the frontiers of that country; of a vile people who as slaves obey the most cruel of all tyrants, a Corsican stained by bloodshed.

Much as one may sympathise with the anguish which Vaudreuil so evidently felt it is a little ironic that he should pray in aid the victories of a *Republican* army and the extension of France's frontiers at the expense of the supporters of the monarchy.

On matters nearer home, Vaudreuil continues,

> Our life is too cruel, and the sorrows of my august friend Monsieur break my heart. We are at this moment about to lose Madame de Polastron who is in the final stage of consumption and who can only be saved by a miracle and we do not see miracles any more in this age of wickedness. I have for the moment left my retreat at Twickenham to give comfort to the poor invalid and to be near Monsieur when he is distressed; for the pleasures of London which drew me there are no more; I am in no state to enjoy them.

While these tragic events were taking place in London and in Paris the backwash of Monsieur's return to Edinburgh in 1801 was making itself felt in Scotland. In 1801 the Home Secretary, Lord Pelham, had given permission to Artois to 'occupy rooms which were inhabited by him in 1796 together with those which belonged to the late Lord Adam Gordon'. Permission had also been given to purchase Lord Adam Gordon's furniture. This prompted a broadside from Lord Breadalbane who wrote directly to Artois demanding the return of his rooms, which was a little unreasonable since he had never occupied them and had, in any case, ceded them long ago to Lord Adam Gordon. Artois had riposted by seeking the help of Chief Baron Dundas, explaining that if Lord Breadalbane's request were met 'the apartments of the late Lord Adam Gordon would be useless and the Royal Apartment would become almost uninhabitable since there would not even be a kitchen for it'. There then followed a protracted bureaucratic wrangle which included the possibility of using the apartments granted to the late Underkeeper of the Palace Dr Moore. The state of play as at 19 May 1802 is contained in a report by Adam Longmoore, the Deputy King's Remembrancer, to the Barons of Exchequer. In this report he agreed that the Duke of Hamilton 'cannot be restricted to less accommodation than he presently possesses'; Lord Breadalbane's apartments had been inspected and found to be 'in a state of great disrepair', and the interest on the capital required to put them in order would far exceed any lodging allowance payable. He went on to say that Dr Moore's lodging has 'entirely been appropriated to the accommodation of His Royal Highness'—Dr Moore, it transpires, was receiving an allowance of £40 per annum in place of his right of occupation. As regards extra lodging demanded for those attending Artois and the Duc de Berry, the Deputy King's Remembrancer was of the view that it would be 'more agreeable to them and less expensive to the public to pay the monthly allowance than to repair and furnish more apartments in the palace'.

It does appear, however, that two other rooms had been fitted up at the expense of the Crown and that later, after Artois's departure, they were made over to the Duke of Hamilton.

From the summer of 1803 the impression is one of the gradual renunciation of Holyroodhouse, of empty rooms and echoing passages, as the former occupants made their way to London or to France. Only the general factotum, Monsieur Pelerin, lingered on at the palace, together with a handful of the nobility with no other refuge such as the Chevalier de Rebourguil, who before the Revolution had been the First Lieutenant of the Alsace Company of Artois's bodyguard, or those too corpulent to move, like the Comte de Coigny.

A watchful civil-service eye was being kept on government property by the King's Remembrancer:

To Monsieur Belville, Exchequer Chambers
No.80 Charlotte Street' 16th August, 1804
Portland Place, London.

Dear Sir,

Upon looking thro' the Royal Apartments last day, I observed that both the carpets and other furniture were spoiling by being exposed to the air, and that it might be advisable to get the furniture washed, and put up till needed—and that the carpets ought to be cleaned and rolled up, but I did not wish to give directions for doing so without mentioning the circumstances to you in case there might be some objection to it, which I am not aware of. I should be glad therefore to know if any objections occur to you to having this done . . .

I am yours, Henry Jardine

M. de Belleville must have assented, since later that year we find instructions being given directly to Pelerin, of which only a handful survive, relating to the moving and storing of furniture, sundry repairs and the care of the garden. Among the repairs required was damage to the drains which, in 1805, were reported as occasioning 'a disagreeable smell'.

Not that all requests by Pelerin were as fruitful as might have been hoped. Perhaps the language barrier prevented complaints being aired with sufficient force. Helpers were to hand:

> Sir
> If you pleas to give orders to mend the chimly on top of the kitchin for it is impossible to leve in it at present—since Satterday all the doors and windows hess to be open for the smock if you pleas to your perticular order for it to be done first
>
> Magrt Johnston for Mr. Pelerin

To this M. Pelerin added an endorsement and the date '30 8bre, 1806'. The kitchen chimney was not the only one to smoke. Madame Pelerin was also having trouble with her bedroom, 'Mrs. Pelerin is sorry to give any trouble to M. Longmoore but thought it was better to mention it now than to wait any longer as things of that kind always grow worse the longer its gets leave to go without repair.' That letter was certainly not composed in English by Madame Pelerin.

The year 1807 saw the authorities disturbed by an unusual request. The Reverend Henry Lloyd, D.D., about whom more deserves to be known and who claimed to be the holder of a Regius Chair at Cambridge, found himself under the necessity of evading his creditors by taking refuge in the Sanctuary. These he intended to repay, perhaps optimistically, from the sale of his projected three-volume historical study of the Old Testament. Having regard to his status as the holder of a Crown nomination he deemed it appropriate that he should be accommodated in the palace itself. Messrs Jardine and Longmoore temporised and the Comte de Coigny and the Chevalier de Rebourguil were consulted. They felt that they could not intervene in an essentially domestic matter but plainly did not relish the company of the impecunious professor. In the end it all seems to have come to nothing.

The same year also saw a flurry of much greater import. Louis XVIII, who was finally driven from Mittau and a subsequent haven near Warsaw, had arrived in England and was granted asylum under the name of the Comte de Lille. The British Government proposed Holyrood as a refuge and went so far as to write to the Lord Provost of Edinburgh instructing him to make the necessary arrangements 'as the Count of Lille and family and suite are expected to arrive immediately'.

Henry Dundas, Lord Melville, once again the *de facto* Secretary of State for Scotland, was alerted at Melville Castle and a frenzy of preparation possessed the palace, but Louis XVIII, perhaps warned by his brother, declined the invitation and settled for Hartwell House, now an elegantly appointed hotel, in Buckinghamshire.

Did Artois ever return to Edinburgh before he left for France in 1814? No trace can be found in the Exchequer records or in the contemporary press. It is not to be excluded that he did return, at least once, and there is some supporting evidence from Lady Clementina Davies. She was born in 1795, a daughter of Lord Maurice Drummond, youngest son of James, Third Earl and Duke of Melfort, members of an important Jacobite family. Part of her youth was spent in Edinburgh and she writes in her reminiscences:

> I was about fifteen years old when in Edinburgh, and I had the opportunity of meeting some very remarkable personages of that day. The Comte d'Artois (afterwards Charles X) was then at Holyrood House, and thither my father frequently took me. The Comte d'Artois was still handsome at the time of his residence at Holyrood, but a dark shadow had fallen on his life; for it was at a then recent date of his long exile from France that he had lost Madame de Polastron, the one woman whom he had loved so well that by the side of her death-bed he had declared to her confessor, the Abbé (afterwards Cardinal) de Latil, that she should never have a successor in his affection.

The circumstantial detail is accurate; she refers elsewhere to the Comte de Coigny 'who had still a very fine face, but who had grown so fat and gouty that he was no longer recognisable in figure as the same man my father had known before the Revolution', but one would wish for further corroboration. If she is correct Artois's Edinburgh visit would have taken place in 1810 or 1811.

The projected arrival of the Comte de Lille in 1807 produced echoes as late as 1811. Among the sparse miscellaneous papers of this period is an 'Estimate of a Superfine Billiard Tablecloth for Holyrood House' by Messrs Broadwood and Cules of Edinburgh at 32/6 per yard. Attached to it is a letter from the Chevalier de Rebourguil to, one may assume, Adam Longmoore:

> Sir,
>
> I had the honour to call twice at your house when you were out. I have a request to present to you. When the arrival of the King of France was announced at Holyrood House you had the goodness to order that billiard tables carpet

should be renewed; but this arrival being postponed you were so good as to promise me that this little repair would take place when the carpet is quite worn out. That is the case now and I then take the liberty to claim your promise and your goodness for the poor invalid inhabitants in the Abbey. The Count de Coigny joins in my request and in the sentiments of gratitude and consideration of

Your most Obedient and humble servant
Rebourguil

This letter is in many ways the epitaph of Holyrood and the first emigration. The Comte de Coigny, companion and *confidant* of Marie-Antoinette, shifts his immense carcass uncomfortably as the east wind creeps round the casements of Holyrood, forces the smoke down the chimneys and spatters rain into the leaking gutters. Of the friends from Versailles, the friends of the early light-hearted days before the emigration, few remain. Gabrielle-Yolande de Polignac is dead; Agläé de Guiche is dead; Louise de Polastron is dead; Armand and Jules de Polignac, Charles-Francois de Rivière, are in prison. The others are now in London. Only a rare visit enables him to hear the gossip and to plan the Restoration which he has awaited for more than twenty years. Charm and manners, dignity and poise remain. Mr Longmoore is thanked with great courtesy for the 'comfortable carpet and the handsome rug'.

For the Chevalier de Rebourguil and the Comte de Coigny, unlike many less fortunate exiles, the long-sought day did at last arrive. Artois entered Paris on 12 April 1814 as the *Lieutenant-Général* of Louis XVIII and in the name of the latter proclaimed an uneasy compromise between those who had gained by the Revolution and the supporters of the divine right of kings, a compromise, unlike that of the following year, weighted in favour of the old regime.

Coigny still remained in Edinburgh, but his eighteen years' residence was drawing to a close. On 5 July 1814 he writes, in French, to the Chief Baron at Arniston.

When you did me the honour of paying me a visit, your lordship saw that I was a mass as heavy as inert, which could not make movements of itself and is in continuous need of being pushed or carried. Fortune, interest, sentiment all call me to France but my difficulty is to get there; my pitiable state forbids me to do so as outside passenger in the coach.

To take an inside seat is too costly. Accordingly he seeks a passage on an Excise ship and, invoking the name of the Duchess of Buccleuch, asks that his wish be granted. Otherwise, he says, 'Shall I ever re-unite myself with my masters, my motherland, my family, my daughter, friends and my future or shall I finish my last days in loneliness, neglect and misery?' This fine Gallic flourish has an illuminating postscript. Even after eighteen years, 'I can neither write nor speak English but I read it as French.'

All is well. The good Chief Baron waves his wand and the voyage is arranged. The Chevalier de Rebourguil pays a farewell visit to Arniston House and, on 22 July 1814, Coigny writes to say that he leaves the following Thursday for Le Havre on the cutter *Oberon.*

His profuse thanks end, 'Long live those who are ungrateful—one never hears from them again when their purpose has been served. Those who are in truth thankful wind up by being tedious.'

With the departure of the last of the *émigrés* the administrators took over. An inventory of the furniture and linen remaining was drawn up—the total value was estimated at £1,774.7.8—and the King's Remembrancer duly reported on 14 January 1815 to the Barons of Exchequer. 'The furniture', he said, 'has been very ill kept and much neglected'. This, he continues,

> was chiefly under the care of a domestic of the name of Pellerin and altho' I believe he was honest yet he and his servants appear to have been negligent and slothful. Notwithstanding I enjoined them frequently to pay attention to the airing and cleaning of the furniture yet upon the whole they have been very careless and remiss and many articles of value, it would appear, have gone on to great decay.

The end of an era, or almost so. In their anxiety to share in the spoils of the Restoration, although they were not to be as lavish as many had hoped, the French nobility forgot some of their more humble supporters in Edinburgh. In 1816 the office of the King's Remembrancer received a petition from Isabella De Taille in which she narrated that she had been appointed by Monsieur to have charge of the royal apartments and 'of shewing them to strangers visiting the Palace'. She asserted that she had been commended to their Lordships of the Exchequer by the Chevalier de Rebourguil who 'had daily access to see and overlook the Petitioner'.

Since the nobility left two years before she had been in charge of the apartments, 'together with the whole of the valuable articles of furniture belonging to the Palace'. The burden of her complaint was that she had received a salary of £50 per annum from Artois but after his return to France she had received nothing. The apartments had been granted to

Colonel Nairne; Madame de Taille had been dismissed and deprived of the only support of her six children. Her husband had already made his way to France and she wished to join him.

From the report on the petition it appears that not only had she lost her salary but also the emoluments from showing visitors around the apartments 'which in some seasons of the year yielded a considerable sum'. The Barons of Exchequer were not persuaded to recognise the vanished income from tips, but granted Madame de Taille the sum of £63 as two years' salary, and she too passes from the stage.

In the rooms a short time before occupied by an exiled court, Caroline Oliphant of Gask, Lady Nairne, the 'Songstress of Scotland', settled at her piano and invoked the memory of another exile. It was not Charles Edward who answered her call of 'Will ye no come back again?', but Charles-Philippe.

CHAPTER 14

Events in France, 1814–30

Artois, as Lieutenant-General for his brother Louis XVIII, entered Paris on 12 April 1814. It was a triumphant entry. The streets were decorated and a *Te Deum* was sung in Notre Dame. Louis XVIII followed on 3 May, once more to scenes of popular rejoicing. Only ten months later, the King and Artois were refugees in neutral Ghent as, in March 1815, Napoleon advanced on Paris.

The second Restoration, after Waterloo, was, in appearance at least, different from the first. Concessions were made to the principles of liberty and equality and the sanctity of property transactions made under the Empire was recognised. Louis XVIII was persuaded to accept as his principal ministers two of the most expert manipulators in Europe, Talleyrand and Fouché, 'vice leaning on the arm of crime', to repeat Chateaubriand's much quoted phrase.

It was not said of the Bourbons that they had 'forgotten nothing and learnt nothing' but of the courtiers surrounding them. None the less the barb pierces. Neither Louis XVIII nor Artois had any belief in parliamentary government. What had sustained Louis XVIII in his years of tribulation was his belief in his own divine right to rule. It could not be expected that he would now change. As for Artois, his position was even more extreme. Had he not said that he would rather earn his living as a wood-cutter than be King of England? While he reigned, however, Louis was a pragmatist, whatever his inner convictions might be. He listened and heeded the advice he was given. Much of the Napoleonic administration was retained, and many of the administrators. Artois accordingly became the focus of the extreme right and the ultra-clerical faction, but at least he remained relatively powerless so long as his brother survived. When, in 1824, Artois became king, the shape of government inevitably altered.

The history of the period between 1815 and 1830 is crucial to an understanding of the development of France in the nineteenth century, but this is a book about Edinburgh, and not about the making of modern Europe. At the same time the importance of the major issues of the period must be outlined, if only to explain the Revolution of 1830, which sent Artois, by then Charles X, once again into exile.

In the first place there were problems of a constitutional nature; the relationship between the Crown and the legislature, the extent of the franchise, and the powers of the elected Assembly. In the second place, and equally important, in that its echoes reverberate today, was the relationship between Church and State, between clericalism and anti-clericalism. As Professor Cobban has put it, 'Napoleon had attempted to use the Concordat [with the Pope] to reduce the Church to the role of an instrument of the State; under the Restoration there seemed a danger that the State might be made an instrument of the Church.' Thirdly, but related to both, was the question of press censorship, rigorously enforced by both Louis XVIII and Artois.

It is also necessary for our narrative to recall one event of a dynastic nature. It had long been apparent that the marriage between Artois's eldest son, the Duc d'Angoulême, and his cousin Madame Royale, the daughter of Louis XVI, would be childless. Louis XVIII had no children. Accordingly the hopes of the monarchy had concentrated on the marriage between Artois's younger son, the Duc de Berry, and Marie-Caroline of Naples, daughter of Francois I of the Two Sicilies. A daughter, Louise, was born in 1819. She subsequently married the Duke of Parma and from them the present-day Bourbon-Parmas are descended, but by the end of 1819 there was as yet no son.

On 13 February 1820, as he was leaving the Paris Opera, then on the site now occupied by the little Square Louvois, just off the Rue Richelieu, the Duc de Berry was mortally stabbed by a paranoiac saddler whose avowed purpose was to extinguish the House of Bourbon. His purpose, however, failed. Marie-Caroline gave birth, on 28 September, to a son, the Duc de Bordeaux, Comte de Chambord and, in monarchist eyes, the future Henri V of France and Navarre—'*l'enfant du miracle*'.

Louis XVIII died on 16 September 1824, after a long and painful illness. At last, Artois, in his sixty-eighth year, 'Monsieur' no longer, came into his own as Charles X of France and Navarre and was crowned in the cathedral of Reims with all the pageantry of his forefathers. It was a near thing. On his journey from Paris he escaped death by a hair's breadth, when his carriage horses, frightened by the noise of a royal salute, bolted, and were only pulled to a halt after twenty minutes. At Reims it was the unassuming son of a concièrge, now Archbishop and soon to be Cardinal, the Abbé Latil, who crowned Artois king, and, according to the faithful, anointed him from the same reservoir of oil as had been used to consecrate Clovis in 481.

Meanwhile, Edinburgh had virtually forgotten its French birds of passage. Some had married into Scottish families. Jules de Polignac, for example had married a Barbara Campbell '*d'Ecosse*'. Others, no doubt, lingered unrecorded, but the great majority had returned to France. Occasionally a face from the past showed up in an unexpected locale. In 1819 Elizabeth Grant of Rothiemurchus and her family made a tour of the Low Countries. At Brussels they received a call from a gentleman her father had known in his youth, 'a good looking, busy-mannered person, with whom the world had not gone altogether well whoever had been to blame for it'. He was most assiduous in his attentions and hoped that they were not being cheated by the local tradesmen. He was more than ready to act as an intermediary. The acute Miss Grant quickly tumbled to the fact that this personable individual was making his living off British travellers by taking a commission from the shopkeepers of Brussels. The commission-agent was none other than Pryse Lockhart Gordon, the former Aide-de-Camp to General Drummond of Strathallan and the life and soul of those early levees in 1796.

For the most part it would also seem that the *émigrés* once returned to France forgot Edinburgh. The anonymous author of *The Hermit in Edinburgh*, published in 1824,—who may have been one Captain Felix McDonough—has a chapter entitled 'A Word about French Emigrants' with the epigraph, 'Freeze, freeze, thou winter sky, thou dost not bite so high, as benefits forgot'. He recounts the tribulations of one, Bob, on a visit to Paris. Bob was

> coarse made, and not overburdened with beauty, plain in his dress, and rough in his address; but a suit of mourning, a glass, pendant at his button-hole, added to gravity and silence amongst strangers, gave him a passport in Paris circles; and although the French people called him John Bull, and *gros patapouf*, [this signifying a great lump of a man], yet they fancied that his pocket was well lined, and they welcomed him, in consequence, in company.

But not all.

> He had seen so many French emigrants in Scotland; He had witnessed the attentions which were paid them—the presents they received, the open doors which awaited them everywhere; the common cant of 'if we ever return to our own country, the English will see how we remember their reception', was so familiar to his ears, that he had pricked down a regular engagement daily, in his memorandum book; but he was mistaken in his men; they scarcely recollected him, he had to put them in mind of his name, his country, day and

hour, place and date, where he had met with Monsieur le Comte, le Marquis, le Baron, le Chevalier, et Monsieur l'Abbé, when he extracted 'O! effectivement, je me souviens d'un certain Robert —— ;' or, in bad English, as if intentionally forgotten, 'Oh! yes. Maister Robert , how do you do, Sir?' and without waiting to ascertain how he could do, in a strange town, 'good *mon-na* ing', pronounced through the nose, and accented as a signal for separation.

According to 'Honest Bob', when he succeeded in making conversation with a former exile his burden was complaint; how badly they had been lodged, how hardly they were treated. 'In a word, every one had a put-off; and some actually passed by old acquaintances, friends and benefactors, unnoticed.'

What mortified Bob the most was,

that some of them were actually receiving half-pay from our government, whilst others had brought away little fortunes from London, which they could not have amassed, but from every door being open to them, and from the warm and generous patronage of our nobility. A certain Countess treated Lady G—— so shamefully, at a party of hers (the emigrant Countess's), that she actually returned to her lodgings, sick with disappointment. Added honours have been given to some of these returned nobles—a step in nobility, a ribbon, or a star; and such is their weakness, whether from age, or debility of mind, or body, that the burden sits so heavily on them that they cannot open a hand, extend an arm, or move a foot to serve an Englishman.

In Edinburgh, the Scots, who, by grant or tradition, had right to quarters in Holyrood, resumed possession. In other cases, new rights of occupancy were accorded by grace and favour. Lady Nairne has been mentioned, but she lived in Holyrood not by virtue of her musical talents but because her husband was His Majesty's Inspector of Barracks in Scotland.

There was, of course, bustle and expenditure when George IV held his receptions and levee there during the famous visit of 1822. Overnight, he preferred the securer comforts of Dalkeith Palace and the hospitality of the Duke of Buccleuch, Walter Francis, grandson of Artois's friend and Angoulême's second mother, the Duchess Elisabeth. The popular tradition that George IV wore pink tights below his kilt seems to have been a myth. According to Basil Skinner, His Majesty wore the kilt only once, and he quotes Harriet Scott of Polwarth as writing that the King wore 'buff-coloured trousers like flesh to imitate his royal knees'.

Charles X did not wholly forget Edinburgh. When, in 1824, a fire caused widespread damage in the Old Town of Edinburgh, he contributed generously to the relief fund.

Charles X however, was, before long, to have good cause to remember Edinburgh. In July 1830 he was summarily driven to abdicate the throne of France. It is difficult to compress the events leading to the Revolution of July 1830 in a few words. It was destined that Charles X would choose ministers from the right, but even a prime minister as reactionary as Villèle consistently found himself outflanked by those even more extreme. After the parliamentary elections of 1827, although based on a narrow suffrage of landed proprietors, Villèle found himself faced with a liberal opposition of almost equal numbers, while the balance was kept by a group of royalist extremists. The latter, for the most part, represented those who felt that the financial provisions made for the returning *émigrés* were wholly insufficient.

Villèle resigned to be succeeded by Charles X's old friend and favourite, the Duc de Polignac,—'Chèr Jules', who had scaled the cliffs of Biville and endured ten years of a Napoleonic prison for his master's cause. No-one could doubt his devotion to Artois, but as Prime Minister he lacked the remotest understanding of the needs of France.

From then on matters ran rapidly downhill. The year 1829 saw the liberal opposition consolidating itself. Despite some initial hesitation, Louis-Philippe, Duc d'Orleans, allowed himself to become the centre of protest supported by a new and influential journal called the *National*. This paper, financed by the banker Lafitte, was the medium by which the ageing Talleyrand was once more manipulating events.

In July 1830 fresh elections were held, giving a two-to-one victory to the liberals. Faced with such a defeat a wiser man than Charles X would have given way and appointed new ministers. Instead Charles X and Jules de Polignac thought that they could dispense with the elected chamber and introduced what were known as the Four Ordinances. These prohibited the publication of any journal of more than twenty-five pages without official approval; they restricted the franchise to the richest twenty-five per cent of the already reduced electorate, and on this basis convened electoral colleges for a new election. The recently elected Chamber was dissolved.

On 28 July rioting began in the streets of Paris, as ever in France the sure barometer of impending constitutional change. By the following day the rioters were effectively in control of the city and Marischal Marmont, the Napoleonic general who was in charge of the Paris garrison, had lost 200 men.

To prevent further catastrophe a group of liberal deputies, together with supporters of Louis-Phillipe, appointed themselves as a municipal council and invited the Duc d'Orleans to become Lieutenant-General of the Kingdom. Only then, and too late, did Charles X react. He agreed to revoke the Four Ordinances, but his overtures were repulsed, and on 31 July he learned that the Duc d'Orleans, on the advice of Talleyrand, had accepted the Lieutenant-Generalcy. Charles X, who by now had abandoned Versailles and retreated to Rambouillet, had no choice left except to accept the *fait accompli.*

On 2 August Charles X abdicated the crown of France, both on his own behalf and on behalf of the Duc d'Angoulême, and instructed Louis-Philippe to proclaim *l'enfant du miracle* as Henri V. Again it was too late. A rabble of about 15,000, reminiscent, as it has often been said, of the march on Versailles of 5 October 1789, had already set out for Rambouillet.

The reign of Charles X was over. Professor Cobban has admirably summarised it in these words:

> The Restoration had failed: this does not prove that it was from the beginning inexorably doomed to failure. On the contrary, the Revolution of 1830 seems at first impression rather the result of a series of accidents, and above all of the obstinacy of Charles X, who went from blunder to blunder as though driven by a blind fate, or as though the little sense there had ever been in that addled pate had entirely vanished with age. He was such a nonentity as to be hardly worth a revolution, and indeed, looking behind the passing events of 1830, one can see that it was not really directed against him; it was against the anachronistic reappearance of a *noblesse* which believed that the eighteenth century had never ended and a clergy which, since the eighteenth century was, so far as the church was concerned, a rather unfortunate episode, looked back to the [seventeenth] century. On the other hand, an important section of the educated classes in France, even if they thought that religion might be good for the masses, did not intend that priests should rule, or that their own sons should be educated by them. They turned against a regime in which the influence of the Church seemed to be increasingly dominant.

Charles X thus began his move westwards, reaching Valognes, just south of Cherbourg, on 14 August. By this time his abdication, without any mention of his grandson, Henri V, had been made public, and the Duc d'Orleans had already appeared before the united chambers of the Assembly and had accepted the crown as Louis-Philippe, King of the French.

On 16 August, at two-thirty in the afternoon, Charles X and all his family left the military harbour of Cherbourg on board the vessel *Great Britain* which was towed by steam tug into the outer basin. Ironically, the *Great Britain* flew the Stars and Stripes, quite properly, since she had been chartered from an American family called Paterson, from which, by a curious twist, came the first wife of Jerome Bonaparte. Why this diplomatic nicety? So that, it was explained, Charles X should not land at Portsmouth under either the tricolour or the Bourbon flag.

One *contretemps* remained. To the consternation of the Government Commissioners appointed to oversee the departure from French soil of Charles X, the *Great Britain* had no sooner made for the open sea than she dropped anchor and a boat was put out for shore. Was Charles X about to renounce his abdication, was he at the eleventh hour seeking to return to Paris at the head of thc largely royalist troops he had just left behind? Nothing so dramatic; those responsible had amply stocked the *Great Britain* with truffles and champagne. They had, however, forgotten the bread.

The voyage was uneventful, but the *Great Britain* had to remain at anchor off the Isle of Wight for nearly a week, while the British Government, in no hurry to show favours to the former King of France, made up its mind what to do with him.

Charles X and his entourage were at last allowed to land and to make their way to the castle of Lulworth, where they had been offered hospitality by Sir Thomas Weld, a member of a family long known for its Jacobite and Catholic sympathies. The second emigration had begun.

Lulworth may have been picturesque enough on a fine August day. The onset of an English autumn revealed that umbrellas were needed indoors as well as out. Worse was to follow. Madame de Gontaut explains why:

> Even in the grounds of the castle, at the turn of a drive, the King found himself stopped by his creditors, the former suppliers of the Army of Condé, who had pursued him in the past. They surrounded him. The King listened calmly and pointed out that their claims had been heard by lawyers in Paris and rejected by the courts as exorbitant. He could only follow the law as it was in fact. They had the cruelty to threaten the King that they would renew their claims. This determined him to ask again from the Court in London the same refuge and privileges which had once before been granted him in Scotland. Dispatches were sent in accordance with his wishes. All was provided with extreme graciousness and sincere interest by the King of England, who felt a strong attachment and respect for the illustrious exile.

The King of England, of course, felt no such thing. George IV had died that summer and there is no record that William IV and Charles X had ever met. What is much more relevant is that Talleyrand, now installed as ambassador to the Court of St James, was encouraging the removal of Charles X from the Channel coast where, according to one of his dispatches to Paris, 'Charles X acted as a pretext for many intriguers to establish themselves by virtue of the easy crossing between France and England'. Talleyrand's wishes prevailed, a naval vessel was provided and Charles X once more set out for the Firth of Forth.

CHAPTER 15

Charles Arrives at Newhaven: Re-established at Holyrood

On 20 October 1830, only a handful of weeks short of the thirty-fifth anniversary of his first arrival, Charles X was once more in Leith Roads. With him, aboard the Admiralty steam-yacht *Lightning*, was the heir to the throne, his grandson, the Comte de Chambord or Duc de Bordeaux, from now on, for the sake of simplicity, referred to as the Duc de Bordeaux. They disembarked about four in the afternoon at Newhaven pier, the baggage having been taken off earlier. The Duc de Bordeaux, said the *Scotsman* in lyrical vein, 'leaped ashore with all the agility of youth and the confidence of innocence'.

The same report added that,

> Charles was cautious, staid in his gait, walked remarkably erect, but there was a shade of gloom in his countenance. 'No man cried God save him, No joyful tongue gave him a welcome back, and Heaven for some strong purpose, steel'd the hearts of the spectators.'

The 'shade of gloom' was understandable. Six months before, Charles X had felt himself secure as King of France, the conqueror of Algiers and master of the Tuileries and Versailles. Now his horizon was the Chain Pier, the fishermen's cottages and the public houses that comprised the Newhaven shore.

This time there was no Commander-in-Chief to welcome the exiled King, no salute of twenty-one guns. Whig policies had little room for fallen monarchs. In Britain, the attitude of mind which would soon express itself in the Reform Acts was gaining ground and presenting a challenge to all established institutions. In France, Louis-Philippe, the Citizen King, represented a more sympathetic form of government. Even Tory opinion hesitated to support the Bourbon cause for fear of provoking a worse reaction. There had even been outbursts of rabble-rousing hostility. Addressing the electors of York, Lord Brougham, characteristically, had spoken of the French nation awaking from an intolerable oppression and expelling a tyrant from the throne which he had dishonoured. Some sections of the Scottish press had been equally hostile, but Sir Walter Scott had come to the rescue. As Lockhart explains,

> among many other things that about this time vexed and mortified Scott, none gave him more pain than to hear that the popular feeling in Edinburgh had been so much exacerbated against the fallen monarch (especially by an ungenerous article in the great literary organ of the place) [*The Edinburgh Review*] that his reception there was likely to be rough and insulting.

Sir Walter, knowing 'his countrymen well in their strength, as well as in their weakness' made a 'touching appeal to their better feelings' in Ballantyne's newspaper for 20 October. The letter is too long to quote in full, but the following excerpts give its flavour. Scott, after a reference to 'the feelings of a Prince under the pressure of misfortunes, which are perhaps the more severe, if incurred through bad advice, error, or rashness,' comes to the heart of the matter:

> It would be unworthy of us as Scotsmen, or as men, if this most unfortunate family should meet a word or look from the meanest individual tending to aggravate feelings, which must be at present so acute as to receive injury from insults which in other times could be passed with perfect disregard. His late opponents in his kingdom have gained the applause of Europe for the generosity with which they have used their victory, and the respect which they have paid to themselves in moderation towards an enemy. It would be a gross contrast to that part of their conduct which has been most generally applauded, were we, who are strangers to their strife, to affect a deeper resentment than those it concerned deeply.

Scott continues,

> Those who can recollect the former residence of this unhappy Prince in our northern capital, cannot but remember the unobtrusive and quiet manner in which his little court was then conducted; and now, still further restricted and diminished, he may naturally expect to be received with civility and respect by a nation whose good-will he has done nothing to forfeit.

According to Lockhart,

> The effect of this manly admonition was even more complete than the writer had anticipated. The royal exiles were received with perfect decorum, which

> their modest bearing to all classes, and unobtrusive, though magnificent benevolence to the poor, ere long converted into a feeling of deep and affectionate respectfulness.

To revert to Newhaven pier, however, where Ballantyne's newspaper would scarcely have had time to circulate, there were no scenes of hostility. Indeed, according to the press report, there were some 'with white cockades in their hats to show respect for fallen greatness'. The most rewarding incident was that recounted in the text which accompanies Kay's *Portraits*:

> Among those that pressed forward to bid him welcome was a jolly Newhaven fishwoman, who pushing everyone aside, seized the hand of the King as he was about to enter his carriage and with a hearty shake exclaimed, 'O, Sir, I'm happy to see ye again among decent folk.'
>
> Charles smiled, and asking her name, she replied, My name's Kirsty Ramsay, sir, and many a guid fish I hae gien ye, sir; and many a good shilling I hae got for't thirty years sin-syne.

According to the *Scotsman*, she followed up her good wishes by pressing half-a-crown into the monarch's hand and Charles, 'not expecting such kindness, unwittingly dropped one of the shillings which rolled across the quay, and was lost in the sea'. The incident ended satisfactorily for all as she was instructed to call at the palace as soon as might be convenient with four hundred oysters.

A less seemly incident occurred at the Palace of Holyrood that night. It had its origins in a dinner for thirty or forty respectable citizens given in Johnston's Tavern, which was not far from the palace, by several of the King's old tradesmen grateful for the patronage which they had received in the past and, no doubt, happily anticipating its renewal. We are again indebted to the *Scotsman*:

> A number of 'loyal and constitutional' speeches were delivered, a number of 'patriotic' songs sung, and about midnight, when 'hot with the Tuscan grape, and high in blood,' the whole party repaired to the palace square, and quite forgetful of the exhausted state of the strangers after their journey, and of their great need for a night's sound repose, and wholly regardless of the sanctity of the midnight hour, they sung that social old Scottish song, 'Should auld acquaintance be forgot'.

The song was led, says the account, 'by a gentleman from Sheffield'. The report adds that 'had it not been for the lateness of the hour, there is a strong possibility that the whole party would have been apprehended, and obliged to answer at the bar of the Police Court for disturbing the public peace.'

It was not an auspicious beginning. Holyrood had had its moment of glory when George IV made his visit to Edinburgh and a guide of 1825 speaks of there having been a 'complete repair' to the palace, but little had changed in thirty years, only that all was more faded, more tarnished and seedy. Margaret Swain tells us 'The royal suite was again dusty and neglected. The furniture, much of it damaged, remaining from 1796 was collected from attics and other rooms. A drawing room was fitted up.' For Charles X and those of his suite who remembered the first exile, when the road from France to Scotland had been so much longer, the contrast between the Tuileries and Holyrood was more immediate and thus the more striking. In 1796 there had been the buffer of six years' travel and hardship between Versailles and Edinburgh. Now, in 1830, Charles X, his circle of friends diminished by death, found himself without the hopes and vision that had sustained him during the earlier visit. In Chateaubriand's graphic image, Charles X 'found the memories of his youth hanging on the walls of the palace of the Stuarts like old engravings, yellowed by time'. Metaphor escalates with the historian. Take, for example, Nettement—'The old Palace of Holyrood, weeping for its kings, made an apt resting-place for the House of Bourbon weeping for its motherland'.

All this is, perhaps, too highly coloured. Charles X had always shown dignity in adversity and fortitude in discomfort, and these virtues come more easily when emotion is lacking. In his seventy-third year all passion was spent; his inconsiderable intellectual grasp still further confined by the formalistic piety instilled so many years before after the death of Louise de Polastron. Contemplation of the hereafter often goes hand in hand with indifference to the present. This, coupled with his habitual inertia, made it almost impossible to interest him beyond his daily whist or the pursuit of game.

'What can one do with such a man?' said Alfred de Damas, the younger brother of the Baron de Damas, Governor of the young Duc de Bordeaux, when they had yet again failed to persuade the King to make a decision regarding the regency of the young prince.

This problem of the regency exercised the whole family in various ways although, in all probability, no-one else. Shortly after his arrival at Lulworth, Charles X had, in a series of letters to the sovereigns of Europe, confirmed his abdication in favour of his grandson. None the less, within the exiled court, he continued to regard himself as the rightful monarch.

The Duc d'Angoulême, who, with his wife and Madame de Gontaut, had arrived in Edinburgh by road, did not associate himself with this correspondence and regarded the abdication of Rambouillet as extorted under duress. If he were not king, he so maintained, he at least should be entitled to the regency of the infant king. Left to himself Charles would have let matters drift, rationalising his lethargy by the explanation that it was essential to preserve the Duc de Bordeaux from the host of place seekers who would proclaim him king before he was of an age to govern.

It required a galvanic shock to arouse the King. That shock, however, was no further away than Bath. The vivacious, attractive and totally impossible, 'that giddy lady', as Sir Walter Scott called her, Marie-Caroline, Duchesse de Berry and mother of the Duc de Bordeaux, was for the time being taking the waters at Bath, her head stuffed with notions of another rising in the Vendée, with herself, a latter-day Joan of Arc, at the head of the leading column which would, as regent, claim the throne of France for her son. Marie-Caroline arrived in Edinburgh in November and, rejecting as unsuitable the accommodation provided for her in Holyrood, betook herself to No.11 (now No.12) Regent Terrace where the Duc and Duchesse d'Angoulême were already installed at No.21 (now No.22). For the Edinburgh fancier who knows Playfair's austerely elegant facade with its incomparable view southwards over Holyrood and the Queen's Park it is an entertaining thought to recall that it simultaneously housed *L'Orpheline du Temple* and the mother of *L'Enfant du Miracle.*

The impending arrival of the Duchesse de Berry caused an unaccustomed flurry of activity on the part of the King since it was rightly surmised that once Marie-Caroline reached Edinburgh no secrets would be possible. At the heart of the discussion was Louis XVIII's former minister, the Duc de Blacas, now, according to unkind critics, the '*Ministre de la nécropole*'. André Castelot has compared him to the master of ceremonies at a high-class funeral and has maintained that his immobile and colourless face well suited the inhabitants of Holyrood and their cast of thought. Blacas did not impress Charles Kirkpatrick Sharpe:

> I'll swear George Sinclair, Sir John's son, who introduced him to me, called him Duke of Black Ass. I have no great *gout* for such people now, and truly this person is not calculated to change one's persuasion. I feel confident from his manner that he was *new*, and enquiries confirmed the impression . . . All the morning, and long he lingered, I thought him anything but civil. However, he was polite enough to steal nothing, and so I wish his dignity good night.

Thanks to Blacas and the imminent appearance of Marie-Caroline, Charles X was persuaded to sign, on 27 November 1830, a declaration again renouncing the crown in favour of the Duc de Bordeaux and investing him with all the rights of kingship. This declaration, however, contained the important reservation that, far from the Duchesse de Berry having the regency, Charles himself would exercise all the rights of regency until his grandson should reach majority, which, in conformity with royal custom, was the age of fourteen, that is to say, 30 September 1833. As a sop to Marie-Caroline the declaration concluded, 'In case it shall please Divine Providence to dispose of us before that date, our well-beloved daughter, the Duchesse de Berry, shall have the regency of the Kingdom.'

It was a close-run thing. Within an hour of signing Marie-Caroline had reached Holyrood and any attempt to conceal from her the content of the declaration failed from the beginning.

The week from 7 to 14 December had the little court in a turmoil. On 8 December it was rumoured that Charles X had changed his mind and intended to adopt another formula by which he would only keep a power to oversee the regency. Alfred de Damas noted in his journal for that day,

> When will he do it? When will he sign it? Certainly his attitude is frank and noble, but will he stick to it? His indecision can perhaps drag on for a month and every month of silence loses his grandson a year.
>
> On 10 December, as I foresaw, he has gone back to the first idea and he has just signed a dozen copies of the first deed. What can one do with a man like that?

On 12 December Marie-Caroline was in full choleric flood—complaining that her serving maid knew all the intentions of her father-in-law and only she was kept in ignorance. Her anger, her determination and her abrasive personality were beginning to take effect. On 13 December, Alfred de Damas notes, 'We have been put off until tomorrow, New uncertainty, Intrigues of all sorts.'

At last on 14 December finality was reached. The Duchesse de Berry would become regent even during the lifetime of Charles X, but only should she land in France.

It is probable that Charles X granted this concession believing it to be of no practical consequence. In this he was wrong, and the adventures of Marie-Caroline thereafter are a story in their own right and one that has often been told. Her departure from the Edinburgh scene was not regretted by Charles Kirkpatrick Sharpe, writing in February 1831:

> I am told that the Dss. of Berry is foolish enough to make people stand up in her presence, which is a great blunder in madame. I saw her in the street, attended by three blackguard-looking men, and very meanly dressed.

It must have been very shortly after this incident that Marie-Caroline left Scotland to reach France by way of the Netherlands, Prussia, Austria and Italy, taking with her the lugubrious Blacas who had been seduced by promises of office under a restored Bourbon monarchy. After months of moving from city to city—only the Duke of Modena gave her the slightest encouragement, and he was generally regarded as being off his head—she and Blacas quarrelled amid the marble dust of Massa di Carrara and the *ministre de la nécropole* returned to his Scottish cemetery, leaving the Duchess to make her way to France without him.

Marie-Caroline arrived in Marseilles in April but the Midi failed her and even the faithful Vendéens could hold out little hope of armed support. In 1799 they had vainly sought a leader in the ranks of the royal family. Now such a leader sought followers in vain. An ineffective uprising against the House of Orleans was swiftly and cruelly repressed and her few supporters killed or scattered. Disguise, betrayal, midnight meetings and moonlight escapes, all the apparatus of a romantic novel, followed in breath-taking sequence. That is, until 7 December 1832 when Marie-Caroline was captured, after a bribe of 50,000 francs had caused her hiding place behind a chimney-piece in Nantes to be revealed once the fire had been lit. Despite her claim, 'Robert the Bruce was defeated seven times before he won the throne of Scotland. I have as much constancy as he', Marie-Caroline had failed. The last pro-Bourbon shot had been fired in France, gaining nothing for the cause of legitimacy and once more leaving a trail of brutality and death in the Vendée. It is easy to condemn Marie-Caroline for risking the lives and happiness of others in a hopeless venture but, given her temperament and romantic aspirations it is difficult to imagine her acting otherwise. 'It was Sir Walter Scott who was to blame,' quotes André Castelot, without giving the source. The comment is surely contemporary with the event.

The affairs of the Duchesse de Berry were not the only matter to trouble Charles X during the early stages of his exile. From the first, rumours were afoot as to the precariousness of his finances. As the *Scotsman* reported, 'We hear that nine carriages bearing the ex-royal arms of France have been arrested in the hands of an expensive coach-maker in Edinburgh.'

Rumour, for once was correct. 'Ocular demonstration', said the *Scotsman*, would vouch its truth. 'The ex-royal carriages are still in durance-vile, and as we stated before, the debt for which they are attached amounts to a pretty considerable sum.'

On 6 November 1830 one François Simon, Comte de Pfaff de Pfaffenhoffen, served at the Palace of Holyroodhouse a summons claiming '446,217 francs, 92 centimes, French money'. Since Charles X had not resided in Scotland for the necessary minimum period to found jurisdiction against him arrestment had been made of carriages belonging to members of the royal suite—the carriages then being in the custody of the coachmaker George Simpson.

Pfaffenhoffen's claim, if true, did not show either Louis XVIII or Charles X in a very favourable light. The Comte Pfaff de Pfaffenhoffen was a native of Germany, resident in Liège and had been employed by *émigré* princes as an agent for furnishing the royal army in 1792. The *émigrés* had set up a printing press for the purpose of manufacturing false *assignats*, the currency of revolutionary France, with which they hoped to undermine the economy. Unfortunately the temptation to use the counterfeit money for their own purchases proved overwhelming. In retaliation, those who had been defrauded succeeded in seizing a large part of the army's baggage train which was in the neighbourhood of Liège. To secure its release Pfaffenhoffen, so he maintained, prevailed upon Monsieur Colson, Mayor of Liège, to advance 160,000 livres to the contractors. To induce Colson to make the advance Pfaffenhausen gave an obligation, both on his own account and as agent for the princes, that the sum advanced would be repaid on the restoration of the monarchy.

Shortly after 1814, Colson's heirs began proceedings in the Courts of Lower Austria and obtained judgment against Pfaffenhausen for the principal sum and interest which then amounted to 249,093 livres. At great sacrifice to himself, so he alleged, Pfaffenhausen paid the debt. Thereafter he applied to Louis XVIII for reimbursement, but although the debt was consistently acknowledged and certain payments to account duly made, much was still outstanding by the date of the July Revolution.

In the defence lodged in the action on behalf of Charles X, the whole incident of the baggage train was questioned, Pfaffenhoffen's mandate was denied and it was suggested that Colson's decree against him in the Austrian Courts had been a collusive one. Moreover, it was said, the personal debt had never been ratified after the Restoration. Any sums due were not owed by Charles X as an individual, but by the French state. While the printed pleadings are extant in the Advocates' Library at Parliament House, it does not seem as if the case ever came to a hearing. The action was still pending when Charles X came to leave Holyrood for last time. It then appears that attempts were made to prevent his departure and security had to be found for the sums claimed. This was obtained from the well-known banker, Sir William Forbes. The action was not finally ended until 14 February 1839, more than two years after Charles' death, when the First Division of the Court of Session pronounced a decree absolving both 'the representatives of Charles X of France and Sir William Forbes, James Hunter and Co and the individual partners thereof.'

Charles X's financial circumstances seem to have been easier than this litigation might suggest. Indeed his generosity to the poor of the Canongate and to the Roman Catholic community in Edinburgh was universally commended, although this generosity was materially assisted by the parsimony which he showed to himself and to those nearest to him.

Moreover, Louis XVIII had, in 1814, by an act of uncommon prescience, deposited the sum of 10 million francs with London bankers against the day when the French monarchy might again have need of it. This sum, plus, no doubt, interest, remained available to Charles X. On the other hand the author of *Souvenirs d'Holyrood*, of whom more later, explains that Charles X had made over to the Duc de Berry all his personal effects, keeping for himself only the life interest. On his abdication all this property had been sequestrated by the government of Louis-Phillipe, an act of vindictive greed in the author's eyes.

There was now a Catholic church at St Mary's, Broughton Street, and a royal pew was fitted up to the right of the altar. There Charles X, clad in a 'blue coat and white trousers and wearing a star', assisted at Mass with the Duc and Duchesse d'Angoulême and the other members of his court. The incumbent was James Gillis, later Bishop Gillis, who had attended a Paris seminary from 1818 to 1823 and who was already known to the royal family. In 1831, armed with letters of introduction from Charles X and his family, Father Gillis made a tour of France, Spain and Italy to gather funds to build a convent in Edinburgh which, in due course, became St Margaret's, Bruntisfield.

The affair of the regency, litigation in the Court of Session and the Sunday church parade seem to have been the total of the King's public life at this time. For the rest, he and his family passed their time in a peaceful, indeed monotonous routine, varied by a round of visits made and received. It is certain that in 1830 Charles X saw his days ending in Edinburgh. As recorded by Miss Knight, the former governess of Princess Charlotte, in her autobiography, Charles X 'said to the Duc de Brissac, "Ah, well, we are here for the second time! We must be quite resigned,

God has willed it," and to the Duchess of Hamilton, he also said, "I meant well, therefore I lay my head peaceably down to rest." '

As will be seen, this intention was to be frustrated in less than two years.

CHAPTER 16

More Perambulations of the King and the Comments of Edinburgh

The inhabitants of Holyrood soon settled to a round of domesticity. The interest of this period lies less in the hopes for another Restoration, although such hopes were never formally abandoned, but rather in the minutiae of existence and the response of the French to Edinburgh and of Edinburgh to the French. At first the movements of Charles X attracted comment in the journals. For example, the *Scotsman* patronisingly reported:

> The conduct of the whole party, since their re-appearance in this city, has given satisfaction to those who have interested themselves in their fortunes. The Ex-King especially, lives strictly retired. When he walks out, he is always accompanied by one or two, or three gentlemen, and appears in the dress of a respectable citizen; he assumes no consequence—he neither courts, fears, nor shrinks from the public gaze, but his whole bearing evinces that he is fully conscious of his misfortunes, and the consequent sufferings they have occasioned. Those who have had opportunities of seeing him, assert that his whole deportment demonstrates that he is conscious that he is fallen from the pinnacle of human greatness, 'never to hope again'.

Charles's perambulations in the town seem originally to have attracted a following, and on one occasion in Hanover Street the crowd became so great that he was compelled to abridge his walk and return to the palace by way of the Mound and the Royal Mile. This attention seems soon to have passed, since on 27 November 1830 Mrs Grant of Laggan writes, 'These Royalties walk about the streets, and lounge in a certain bookseller's shop. This person is a favourite, the king having known him thirty years since, when he was at Holyrood. I hear a great deal about them, and all I hear is in their favour.'

The King came in for a certain amount of banter from the 'keelie-boys' or street arabs of the Canongate when he emerged from the palace to shoot snipe in Hunter's Bog on the flank of Arthur's Seat, 'Frenchy, Frenchy, dinna shoot the sprugs', but there is no suggestion that he took it amiss. Almost certainly, he totally failed to understand what they were saying.

For the most part Charles X's expeditions were to neighbouring lairds. He and the Duc d'Angoulême sometimes crossed the Forth by the ferry at South Queensferry to visit the Trafalgar veteran, Admiral Sir Philip Durham, at Fordel, but more often they were the guests of the Earl of Wemyss at Gosford. Lord Wemyss had known Charles X in Paris and the Baron de Damas, Governor to the Duc de Bordeaux, paints an attractive picture of his being re-introduced to his old friend, '*évidement un grand seigneur*', but so lame that he could only walk with help. 'After that, he his wife and children, in short the whole family, were from then on those that we saw the most.' All the Wemyss family spoke French faultlessly and, for once, Damas felt completely at home, On one such visit Francis Steuart recounts being told by an eye-witness, then over ninety, of the exchange, 'Why is yon auld gentlemen ca'ed Charles X?'—'Jist because he's ex-King of France.' There were also expeditions to the Hopes of Craighall and to Pinkie where, until at least the beginning of this century, there was, in pride of place, a stuffed bird labelled, 'Shot by the Comte d'Artois', although given the style and title of the marksman one wonders whether it was not a souvenir of an earlier visit. The species of the bird is not recorded. At Dalmeny, the home of the Earls of Rosebery, on one occasion, the bag was thirty-six pheasants, besides hares and partridge—large for those days, and a useful addition to the frugal commissariat of Holyrood.

The *Memoires* of the Baron de Damas are one of the principal sources of our knowledge of this period, and their author merits description. For Madame de Boigne he represented the '*Congrégation* incarnate'. The *Congrégation de la Foi* was the most extreme secular wing of the Catholic Church in France. Many of those around Charles X belonged to it, although membership was as often as not concealed. The appointment of Damas as Governor to the Duc de Bordeaux had been made, in 1829, by Charles X himself, provoking yet another constitutional dispute, since the Royal Council not unreasonably thought that they should have a say in the upbringing of an heir apparent and the Baron de Damas would certainly not have been their choice. His father had emigrated in 1789 and was subsequently killed in the Quiberon landing. The Baron was found a place in the St Petersburg Military Academy, did well in the Russian army and, after the Restoration, served both Louis XVIII and Charles X as a minister. He is sometimes described as unintelligent but that was not the case. Unimaginative, bigoted and humourless he may have been, but within the limits imposed by his rigid premises he was intelligent enough. The tone of his *Memoires* may be condescending but they are the work of a literary stylist.

He is not enamoured of Holyrood, 'good enough for a private citizen', but not as the residence of a monarch. He is scathing about the furniture, 'a few old pieces of mahogany covered with printed cotton' (*en indiennes communes*), curtains of the same material, old paper on the walls and the staircases poorly whitewashed. He adds that, 'This simplicity, which is in marked contrast to our habits, meant no disrespect to Charles X. The King of England lived there when he came to Edinburgh; the private houses of the Emperor of Austria and many other princes are scarcely better furnished and we consider that the Bourbons are an exception in this respect.' Arthur's Seat and the King's Park do not impress him, 'not a tree', but he refers to the Duke of Hamilton's right to quarry stone from which are built 'the most handsome houses of Edinburgh. Despite the climate they conserve their natural colour which is that of old Roman monuments toasted by the sun of the Midi.' It is now not easy to imagine the colour of the New Town when it was first built.

One may, perhaps, forgive the Baron de Damas for his jaundiced view of Holyrood. He explains that the palace had been divided into a number of apartments and that this was most inconvenient:

> My bedroom was behind that of the king; it gave on to the courtyard, was large and fine, but it served as a passage, not only for the princes, but also for the public, that is to say those visiting the palace. This was some sort of right of way, and the local authorities, thinking that it would be difficult to suppress it all at once asked us to be patient. But one can judge how much this communal living inconvenienced me. Later I was more suitably lodged. My sitting-room adjoined the anti-chamber of the Duc de Bordeaux; I had a bedroom and a *cabinet de toilette.*

A military guard was provided, 'twelve or fifteen Scotsmen commanded by a sergeant', and the civic authorities paid their respects, 'but always on a personal footing. Anything which might resemble the honours due to a sovereign was avoided'.

From the Baron de Damas we can reconstruct the royal household, but the details of grandiose titles bereft of content are not of great interest. The Duc de Polignac, whose unfortunate brother, Jules de Polignac, was still incarcerated in France, was in charge of the household and 'M. O'Hégerthy', senior, was in charge of a few horses or, 'more properly, the royal stables'. The Abbé Joquart was confessor to the King assisted by the Abbé de Bourdeille. The Baron de Damas was assisted in his duties as Governor to the Duc de Bordeaux by Monsieur de Barbançois and Monsieur de Maupas, about whom we know little except that they played Box and Cox, one always being in France. In due course the Cardinal Latil, now 'De' Latil according to the *Memoires*, the unassuming *curé* having risen socially as well as ecclesiastically, arrived in Edinburgh. Only the inner circle were lodged in the palace itself; the remainder were lodged in houses nearby.

Shortly after his arrival Charles X took a lease of Baberton House at Juniper Green, only a few miles from the centre of the city, and which then belonged to a Mr Archibald Christie. The house dates from 1622, with eighteenth-century additions and alterations. One of the principal bedrooms is, or was, known as the 'King's Room' and has a ceiling decorated with *fleur-de-lis* in honour of the King. Francis Steuart says that the reason for the lease was for the sake of Charles's grandchildren, the Duc de Bordeaux and the Princess Louise, so that they could be out of the way of political attacks, 'which were stirred up by the intrigues of the Duchesse de Berri'. This seems unlikely. In November 1830 the Duchesse de Berry had yet to embark upon her extravaganza and the Baron de Damas provides a more convincing reason:

> It was the time of cholera: it was wide-spread in Paris and appeared in the outskirts of Edinburgh. We thought of transporting the royal family some distance from the town. A small country house was leased but we did not establish ourselves there; the cholera disappeared from Edinburgh without having done much harm. The country house served us as a place of rest and recreation.

At a personal level the Baron de Damas made many friends, largely from the Tory aristocracy and landed proprietors—the names of Hope, Dundas and Wedderburn are often mentioned. Others included Admiral Durham, the Sir Phillip Durham of Fordel, already mentioned; the distinguished diplomat Sir Robert Liston and a certain Mr Robinson, 'amiable and witty, who had made his fortune in the Indies and who often had me to dine; he acted as our guide when we visited the curiosities of the neighbourhood.'

The 'Mr Robinson' can be identified as John, later Sir John, Robison, who had indeed made his fortune in the service of the Nizam of Hyderabad, but in 1830 had long retired and was the efficient and inventive General Secretary of the Royal Society of Edinburgh. It was said of him, in the *Dictionary of National Biography*, 'from boring a cannon to drilling a needle's eye, nothing was strange to him. Masonry, carpentry and manufacture in metals were almost equally familiar to him. His house in Randolph Crescent was built entirely from his own plans, and nothing, from the cellar to the roof, in construction or in furniture, but bore testimony to his minute and elaborate invention.' John Robison also spoke French fluently.

All this suggests that Damas had interests outside exclusively court circles. The Baron adds that their banker was 'M. Forbes', that is to say the eminent and aristocratic Sir William Forbes, and, as if to excuse himself for moving in such circles, he explains that the Monsieur Forbes 'belonged to the powerful family of Lord Forbes. One knows that in England the younger branches do not scorn to enter the world of finance or commerce'.

That Edinburgh made the exiles welcome is confirmed by Mrs Grant of Laggan:

> My passion is to see the Duchess of Angoulême. I have for many years cherished a mournful admiration of that long-enduring heroine of calamity: I revere her piety, and honour her deep and undisguised filial affection. The Whigs here, taking up the tone of the French, whom they delight to glorify, say that she has an unpleasant expression of countenance—quite a scowl: I tell them she rises in my estimation by not concealing that virtuous indignation, the impression of which on her firm and noble mind must be indelible.

Mrs Grant, by all accounts the most generous of persons, combined both faith and works:

> . . . last week three of the most beautiful snow-white ptarmigans came; they had already thrown off their summer dress and were milkwhite, with the exception of rich scarlet eyebrows. I could not think of eating the beauties myself, and immediately destined them for the Duchess, lodging them in a slight little basket, and sending them with a Highland porter, with orders merely to hand them in to the servant and to come away; which was done.

The royal grandchildren and their education, temporal and spiritual, were the focus of the household. The Duc de Bordeaux had been promoted from the care of Madame de Gontaut, but she was still nominally in charge of 'Mademoiselle', the Princesse Louise. Many people in Edinburgh thought that Madame de Gontaut was seeking to marry Charles X and, like the Duc de Blacas, she incurred the displeasure of Charles Kirkpatrick Sharpe who wrote, in August 1832:

> It is reported that the King of France is going to marry Madame de Gontaut who rules the roast [sic] already. Here is a new Madame de Maintenon, full as clever but not *quite* so pretty.

Many years later, writing of the Duc de Bordeaux, he said:

> There is one thing I never could forgive Madame de Gontaut and his other attendants for, and that is the neglect of one of his ankles, who had gone quite wrong when I saw him as a boy. Madame, I'll warrant you had other fish to fry than to mind such trifles. Of all the people I knew (and much I saw of her at Lady Hampden's), I had the worst;—but I am wandering out of my way to be scandalous.

As indeed he was. Within the bizarre limits thought appropriate for the education of royal children, she provided continuity and kindness and had endured much on their behalf. It seems, certainly, that there was some temporary coolness which led to Madame de Gontaut's leaving Edinburgh for a spell. In her Memoires she put it down to a form of nervous breakdown due to the separation from her own children: 'I fell into a state of languor which gave concern to those around me and it was thought that I could not safely occupy myself with the education of Mademoiselle. The King gave me leave, and thanks to the skill of Dr. Abercromby and two months rest at Lady Hampden's, I recovered completely.' She hurried back to Edinburgh for the first communion of Mademoiselle of which something more must be said. Whatever difficulties there may have been, Madame de Gontaut was one of the few survivors from Versailles and had known Charles X at all stages of his life. She, and the Cardinal 'De' Latil, represented continuity as did few others.

Miss Felicia Skene was the youngest daughter of James Skene of Rubislaw, Advocate for Charles X in the Pfaffenhausen affair, historian, a close friend of Sir Walter Scott and a distinguished amateur artist. Writing in 1895, Felicia Skene tells how, since her parents knew Madame de Gontaut, she was chosen to play with the Duc de Bordeaux and Mademoiselle. 'The Duc de Bordeaux was somewhat more carefully guarded than his sister, so we chiefly met him in the palace; but Mademoiselle was allowed to come and spend many happy days with us in our home,' Even then poor Princesse Louise was conscious of her heredity since she 'often speculated in the quaintest manner as to what her own fate was likely to be—whether she was to find herself on some European throne, or in neglected obscurity'.

In fact she fulfilled both destinies. Married to the Duke of Parma, Duchess regnant after his assassination in 1854, she was deposed in the Italian Revolution of 1860 and died in neglect in 1873 and was interred in what had by then become the family vault in Goritz, nowadays just inside the Slovenian border, of which Charles X was to be the first Bourbon occupant.

This 'bright, vivacious child full of intelligence', as Miss Skene describes her, could even turn her rank to play:

> We would vary our amusements from hide-and-seek and other games to the arrangement of a mimic court, in which Mademoiselle was perched on a throne formed of cushions piled upon the table, while we acted as ladies in waiting.

Even in Edinburgh, however, danger lurked.

> Mademoiselle's visits to our house [in Princes Street] came to an abrupt and painful end by the dastardly action of a French revolutionary, who waylaid her as she was alighting from her carriage at our door, and heaped curses on all who bore the name of Bourbon with the fiercest invectives. Her governess, with the help of our butler, succeeded in hurrying the terrified child into the house and closing the door on the miscreant, who would have followed, but poor Mademoiselle came flying into the drawing-room sobbing out her indignation and terror, '*Il a dit des injures de mon grandpère*,' ['he has said horrible things about my grandfather'], she repeated over and over again as we tried to pacify her, and it was sometime before she recovered her composure.

After that, all the meetings took place at Holyrood, and Felicia Skene tells another story which demonstrates the blend of claustrophobia and naïveté which permeated the *émigré* court. The game was a form of charades. A word was given, 'courtship', and the children had to draw the syllables. The prize was a drawing by Monsieur d'Hardiviller, the drawing master:

> The scene is before me now, The Duc de Bordeaux, a quiet fair-haired boy, laboriously setting to work in perfect silence; Mademoiselle full of animation and excitement, talking rapidly in French, and expressing the hope of winning the coveted prize. I was the youngest child in the room, and my attempts must have been of the crudest description. What I made of the court scene I do not

> remember, but when it came to the ship I portrayed, I added a flag which was about twice the size of the ship itself. Then it occurred to me that my conspicuous banner would be the better of some ornamentation, so I drew some flowers upon it, entirely the offspring of my own fancy. When the finished drawings were collected for judgement, my flowery flag instantly attracted the attention of the loyal French exiles, and the universal cry arose, '*les fleurs-de-lis! les fleurs-de-lis!* The dear sympathetic child has drawn the *fleur-de-lis* in honour of France!'

So Miss Skene was duly awarded the prize despite the fact that 'I knew nothing about the *fleur-de-lis*, and that no sentiment towards France had inspired me in executing the meaningless hieroglyphics on my flag'.

The education of the Duc de Bordeaux was altogether more rigorous. Rising at six he was taught French, Latin and history by Monsieur Barrande, with 'a zeal worthy of the greatest praise', says de Damas. We know little of Barrande except that de Damas adds that his temperament was correct and inflexible, (*droit et raide*) and that subsequently his head was turned by excessive praise from Chateaubriand. Drawing was taught by Charles-Achille d'Hardiviller and English by a Mr Black, an 'excellent man and a good royalist' who had at one time lived in France. As might have been expected de Damas was much concerned with the religious education of his ward and sought a Jesuit preceptor but, interestingly enough, this was refused by Charles X and later, when the court in exile had moved to Prague, it was Damas's insistence on Jesuit tutors which provoked his downfall.

There was, happily, a lighter side. Damas and the Duc de Bordeaux, no doubt aided by John Robison, made a series of excursions to see the sights of Edinburgh, rather it would seem in the spirit of an explorer venturing into the uncharted wastes of Africa. 'Edinburgh offers to the curious much to remember, a population and way of life to which we were not accustomed. All that could only make a valuable impression, on a child certainly, but a child whose intelligence was greatly ahead of his age.'

Accordingly, there were visits to *l'Académie*, by which must be intended the University, since they there saw experiments in physics, the like of which they had never seen before; the Archives, 'admirably maintained and protected'; the Advocates' Library; the prison, which was clean and well ventilated but where the food was poor by French standards. They saw 'establishments founded for the poor', factories, barracks and the troops at drill; they even enrolled in the Royal Company of Archers. At the schools they attended '*exercises*', that is to say gymnastics, and often watched boxing. This latter must have taken place at the schools, since it is difficult to imagine de Damas exposing his charge to the crowd surrounding professional pugilists. As with the Capitaine de Boisgelin, Heriot's school receives a special mention. 'There 300 or 400 children of the people are maintained free of charge and are very well educated'. Other schools also provided education of a sort for poor children. They lacked however the virtues of a Catholic seminary.

> These benefits are, doubtless, useful and good. They could not be wholly so unless they rested not just on the generous spirit of their benefactors, but on a religious foundation. Such a foundation does not exist, everyone does what he wants and in the way he chooses, the sects being without number and, particularly in Scotland where presbyterianism dominates, it comes down to the religion of Mr. So and So, who is the master of his own church.

Scottish sabbatarianism equally displeased De Damas:

> In this country, however, at the time I was there, the Sunday day of rest was observed by everyone with extreme rigour, to the point that one day, after church, when my prince was shooting with his bow in the private garden of the Palace, he was seen from a neighbouring hillside and there was a public scandal. I had to apologise and promise not to do it again.

The informal visits had to be curtailed, however, after the unpleasant episode involving Mademoiselle, and the excursions had to be made by carriage and, even then, to some secluded house such as Dalmahoy Park, where the Duc de Bordeaux could play with the young sons of the Earl of Morton. Indeed, if Miss Knight is to be believed, 'four persons were sent from Paris to take the life of the Duc de Bordeaux' but found him too well guarded.

As might be expected the first communion of the Princesse Louise and the Duc de Bordeaux were events of importance. The former took place during the spring of 1831. It will be recalled that Madame de Gontaut had hurried back to Edinburgh for this ceremony which, she tells us, was conducted by the Abbé Busson, 'who, for this important act, left his position at the archbishopric', which post she does not say, 'and sacrificed his position with the most noble lack of self-interest. From that moment on, his career was shattered; he retired to his birthplace, and there, still today, amid the poor whom he comforts and the deaf-mutes whom he teaches, he dedicates his fine intelligence to his fellow-creatures'. It was thus, that the Orleans took their revenge.

The first communion of the Duc de Bordeaux, which took place on 2 February 1832 at St Mary's was altogether a more elaborate affair. A record of the occasion still exists in the Cathedral treasury in the form of a monstrance, suitably inscribed, which was presented by the communicant. All went without a hitch but the day was not otherwise marked and the young man at the centre of the occasion was not even given the rest of the day off.

The Baron de Damas records,

> There was nothing special in the Palace and we continued with our daily routine. As always I insisted that the prince write his diary or rather the scrutiny of his conscience; therein his noble soul often manifested itself in sublime outpourings. [*Son âme élevée s'y manifestait souvent par des élans magnifiques.*]

Poor Henri, Duc de Bordeaux and Comte de Chambord, aged 13. The laying on of hands and administration of the sacrament was performed, it need hardly be said, by the omnipresent Cardinal Latil.

This chapter, accordingly, may suitably end with a view of Latil through Scots eyes. The narrator is, once again, Mrs Grant of Laggan, and she reports, on 13 November 1830, what Robert Miller, the bookseller, told her of the 'clerical retinue of the ex-royal family of France':

> He had formerly known the king's confessor here, but had not a distinct notion of his added dignities, further than that he was Archbishop of Rheims. He called at Holyrood, and found a whole conclave of the priesthood. The prelate, after the kindest possible welcome, presented him to the Duke d'Angoulême's confessor, then to the Duchess's, then to the guardian of the Duchess of Berri's conscience. The Archbishop was seated, and the rest with due humility, stood in his presence till he bid them be seated. Miller watched their mode of expression, to modulate his own by it. One asked if his Eminence wished for more air; upon which Miller asked if his Eminence had walked out much since his arrival. He is, it seems, a cardinal,—the first of those princes of the church who has been in Scotland since the memorable days of Cardinal Beaton. It is now rumoured that the Ex-Dey of Algiers is coming to Edinburgh: if so, he may address the ex-king in a manner that I thought still more applicable to Buonaparte's arrival among the shadowy sovereigns of ancient days:—'All they shall speak and say, Art thou also become weak as we,—art thou become like one of us?' What a solemn and awful passage this is, in the fourteenth of Isaiah!—One grows dizzy in looking at this whirl of alteration.

CHAPTER 17

Varied Impressions: Last Days in Edinburgh and Departure for Prague, 1832

The savage suppression of Marie-Caroline's up-rising in the summer of 1832 made it clear to the other kingdoms of Europe, if it was not clear already, that the white flag of the Bourbons would never again fly in France. Such half-hearted and conditional support as there had been fell by the way. Only those closest to Charles X retained their fantasies. In his *Mémoires* the Baron de Damas maintained that 'the almost unanimous disposition of the [European] governments would have offered to us a powerful and glorious rescue if we had known how to take advantage of them, but all our desires were rendered nugatory by the unbelievable inertia of the king and by the divisions which split the family and those advising them.' Damas was at least correct in his presentation of Charles X. The impression is irresistible that from the moment of his first act of abdication Charles X had lost all personal desire to rule and had reconciled himself to exile, preferably in the tolerable surroundings of Holyrood. He may have dreamt of the restoration of the Duc de Bordeaux as Henri V, but he himself had lost the will to bring it about. He and the Duchesse d'Angoulême were frightened by Marie-Caroline's campaign and only desired her return to her children. Charles X wrote to her in August 1832, when, unknown to him, Marie-Caroline was already in hiding in Nantes:

> I take advantage, my dear child, of a safe messenger to express to you the deep anxiety which I feel for your brave but useless perseverance in an undertaking which lacks principle and which cannot be other than dangerous for you and disastrous for the cause which we uphold.

He tells her that he writes with the express approval of the Duc and Duchesse d'Angoulême and begs her to return to him, where she will find 'among us all the affection which we have never ceased to feel for you'. Even if the latter phrase was an exaggeration the message is clear.

That is not to say that Charles X was not subject to pressure by the few remaining monarchists. During the first year, at least, of the second exile there were many who sought to visit Holyrood, each with a scheme more impracticable than the one before. For the most part Charles X wished to have nothing to do with them and the Baron de Damas did his best to prevent their making the journey to Edinburgh.

One visitor, on the other hand, was made very welcome. Raimon Desèze, a star of the Bordeaux bar, had been the youngest and most effective of Louis XVI's counsel. He survived the Revolution, was made Comte de Sèze, thus gaining the magic particle, a peer of France and President of the re-established Cour de Cassation, the highest appeal court in France. He had died in 1828 and this was now his son, another Raimon, who came to pay his respects. He visited Edinburgh in both May and November 1831 and recorded his impressions on both occasions in his *Souvenirs d'Holyrood.* It is difficult in translation to capture the tone of his besotted adulation of the royal family, and in any case a little goes a long way. In passing it may noted that Raimon de Sèze stayed at the Black Bull in Leith Street 'which is excellent *pour les amis de Charles X*, to quote the young and pretty niece of the innkeeper, who speaks good French'.

Of the palace he has this to say:

> Holyrood is a vast palace, situated at one of the extremities of the old town of Edinburgh; an open space separates it from the foul and melancholy suburb of the Canongate. On all sides it is surrounded by mountains: that which overlooks it to the left is crowned by the most elegant and picturesque of buildings, and girdled in part by houses which are new and light in colour. One of these houses is occupied by Madame la Dauphine; another by Madame [i.e. the Duchesse de Berry] during her stay in Edinburgh . . . The apartments of Charles X, who in spite of his abdication, is here always called *le Roi*, are plain but spacious. A fine ante-chamber, two salons and a billiard room comprise the reception rooms, and the hospitality of the King of England is as worthy of the prince who grants it as the prince who receives it.

He gives an account of his first visit to the king. It was a non-event by most standards, but it demonstrates the sterile formality by which the ageing and isolated group regulated their days:

> At half past nine, then, we presented ourselves to Monsieur the Duc de Blacas. His friendly welcome would have set us at ease should we have had need of it. At eleven o'clock, at his behest, we entered the salon of Charles X, where were gathered together Mgr Le Dauphin, Mme La Dauphine, Mgr the Duc de

> Bordeaux, Mademoiselle and all the faithful courtiers who had followed the princes to a foreign land. Already the warmth of what was said would have rewarded us amply for our journey but, after Mass, Charles X summoned us to his study. At the end of the conversation, during which the clock alone revealed to us how quickly time had passed, he did us the honour of an invitation to dinner. At six o'clock we found ourselves once again in the salon of Charles X; we passed the evening in his presence and at ten o'clock the party dispersed.
>
> During all that day while question followed upon question and conversation filled every moment not a word of bitterness fell from the lips of the princes. They wished to know everything and condemned none. It was an excess of generosity which seemed to me to be beyond the bounds of nature.

Charles X is described as 'a model of goodness, charm and dignity. His attitude is that which one would wish it to be; conscientious but calm and noble'. There is perhaps a hint of criticism in de Sèze's reference to the Duc d'Angoulême, 'This prince so misunderstood, this son so devoted, this subject, Alas! so obedient.' Did he feel that Angoulême could have been more active in the royal cause?

It is only with the Duchesse d'Angoulême, *la Dauphine*, that the pen-portrait gains a third dimension.

> Mme the Dauphine, who at Lulworth bore her unhappiness with such courage, seemed to me sad and in low spirits; memories never cease to pursue her. One is afraid to speak of France to her and it is of France she continually speaks . . . She sought the news of all her friends, for it is thus she calls them. There were names which she could not pronounce without tears; then when the conversation turned to people and events where it was impossible to refrain from condemnation she became silent and wept no more.

Romain de Sèze had little time to see the sights of Edinburgh, but on 9 May 1831 he had a day free of engagements and explored the town. He found much to admire in Edinburgh, an 'astonishing admixture of Greek buildings and Gothic churches which only yesterday had emerged from the mason's chisel'.

One passage allows us to see the New Town through Parisian eyes:

> Imagine to yourself, that you may have some feeble idea of it, a street as broad as the Rue de la Paix, of immense length, ending at the flank of a green hill which wears like a crown a cluster of columns and which is surmounted by a picturesque monument to Nelson. At the end of this street, at the part called Waterloo Place, you find two gateways of a rich architectural style. You

> approach and see with surprise but without fear that you are standing on a bridge of prodigious height. You look below you and see flowing, not a river, not a torrent, but, to use an expression which alone can paint the sensation one feels, you see flowing a constant current of people. The street below resembles a dry ravine in which one has built on each side a row of houses so that their top storey forms the ground floor of those which surround you.

He contrasts the splendour of the New Town with the squalor of the Canongate, 'inhabited by the poorest and dirtiest of Edinburgh's population.' He is struck by the 'young girls, carefully wrapped in their large cloaks but bedraggled, running bare-foot on the cold paving stones and slipping on wet footways.'

By the spring of 1832 it was becoming evident for one reason or another that, contrary to his personal wishes, Charles X's second exile in Edinburgh was reaching an end. Relations between the British Government and Louis-Philippe were becoming closer as month succeeded month and as the latter consolidated his control of France. Talleyrand's embassy to the Court of St James had proved fruitful and, although nearing eighty, his charm was as effective as ever and his cunning as supple. His acceptance by the London establishment is epitomised by the special handrail, still in place, which the Travellers Club fitted to their main staircase to allow the crippled ambassador to make his way to the dining-room on the first floor. Logically these factors should have led to governmental pressure on the royal exiles to leave Edinburgh, and one view is that it was to avoid such an indignity that Charles X began to negotiate an alternative asylum. This was certainly the view of the Duke of Wellington. In a letter dated 28 September 1832 to the politician and man of letters, John Wilson Croker, he wrote:

> I am inclined to believe that the retreat of Charles X from Edinburgh was a measure of prudential anticipation, on his part, of a course which he conceived was to have been presented to him in a short period of time. He saw clearly that he had no hope of protection from the ministers, and he anticipated the *invitation* which they would receive to send him away.

There is an another view, and one which accords more closely with Charles's obstinate temperament. In fact it suited Talleyrand very well to have the ex-king in Scotland where he was near enough to be effectively supervised and yet far enough away to do little direct harm. Talleyrand's scheming to this effect was known at Holyrood and it was to avoid being so manipulated that Charles X felt he had no option but to resume his travels. In any event, the Emperor of Austria was approached, and Gratz in Styria was suggested. At first the Emperor was reluctant to give his consent. He, too, against his personal inclination, was seeking a *rapprochement* with Louis-Philippe. The Emperor had been sheltering *l'Aiglon*, Napoleon's heir. *L'Aiglon* had just died, however, and it was a convenient moment to repair the bridge with France. In the end, blood was thicker than water and the Emperor agreed in principle to provide a refuge for the Bourbons.

Accordingly, in August 1832, Charles was able to thank formally His Majesty King William IV for his hospitality and to announce his imminent departure for Austria.

While these negotiations were taking place it was decided that the Duc de Bordeaux needed to be removed from the conspiratorial atmosphere of Holyrood and distracted from the anxiety caused by the disappearance of his mother into the alley-ways of Nantes. In July, therefore, he made a tour of the Highlands in the company of the Baron de Damas, Messieurs Barrande and de la Vilette and the drawing master, d'Hardiviller. The latter has left a handsome volume illustrating the tour. They progressed by Lochleven where they saw the castle where Mary Queen of Scots had been imprisoned; they visited Fort William and the battlefield of Culloden and the castles of the Dukes of Argyll and Hamilton. Francisque Michel quotes an account of how at one halt in this journey the Duc de Bordeaux was greeted by a large gathering of Highlanders wearing the white cockade. This greatly alarmed De Damas and the others. They pictured themselves as the involuntary leaders of another Jacobite rising, but the Duc de Bordeaux, it seems, rose to the occasion, found suitably anodyne words, and the party retreated hastily to the nearest town.

Despite the agreement of the Emperor the ultimate destination of the royal exiles remained unclear and it was decided to send the Duchesse d'Angoulême to Vienna as a *fourrier* or harbinger to see what specific offer she could extract from the Emperor who was, after all, her cousin. Thus it was that, to quote Francis Steuart,

> On 15th August 1832 the Duchesse d'Angoulême presented locks of the hair of all the members of the royal family to their staunch friend, the Rev. James Gillis, afterwards Bishop of Limyra, and also two beautiful bronze statuettes of her father, King Louis XVI, and her mother, Queen Marie-Antoinette. These now decorate the Ursuline Convent of St Margaret, at Bruntisfield, to which convent they were bequeathed by Bishop Gillis, the Duchess having desired that they should always remain in the hands of her co-religionists.

The Duchesse d'Angoulême reached London about 10 September, having travelled by road. There she was joined by Mademoiselle, the Princesse Louise, and Madame de Gontaut who, resignedly, remarks, 'As ever we left not knowing where we were going'. In London the Duchess received a private visit from the Queen and said farewell to a number of friends. Then, by way of the ordinary packet-boat to Rotterdam, she reached Vienna where she was able to send to her father-in-law the good news that the Emperor had agreed to the temporary use of part of the vast Hradschin palace—said to have 400 rooms—at Prague.

In the meantime Tuesday, 18 September, had been fixed for the departure of Charles X, the Duc d'Angoulême and the Duc de Bordeaux. The government had grudgingly promised the use of its steam-packet *Lightning* which had conveyed Charles X to Edinburgh two years before. *Lightning* in fact did not arrive until 20 September, and, in the interval, the king had, in exasperation, chartered the merchant ship *United Kingdom* for the voyage to Hamburg. The ceremonies of farewell spread themselves over several days.

The text accompanying Kay's *Portraits* tells us much:

> When it became known that the royal exiles were on the eve of their departure from Edinburgh, a general feeling of regret was manifested by the inhabitants . . . On the Saturday previous, the tradesmen, who had been employed by the ex-royal family, entertained the members of the household at dinner in Millar's tavern. In reply to the expressions of regret for their departure, the Frenchmen said, 'they regretted the separation, the more especially as they had just been long enough here to form friendships, which were now to be torn asunder. If they did not return to France, there was no place on the face of the earth where they would be more anxious to remain than at Edinburgh.'

On the Monday there was presented an address 'from a considerable portion of the inhabitants' and suitably high-flown sentiments were exchanged. Early on the Tuesday a further deputation waited on the King to present another address. They were led by the Lord Provost and included John Menzies of Pitfodels who had given his estate of Blairs in Aberdeenshire to the Catholic church for the education of priests, John Robison, the Secretary of the Royal Society of Edinburgh and Dr Browne, Advocate, who was the author of the address. This, according to Kay, subsequently excited a great sensation, 'both in this country and on the Continent'. If it did, posterity has drawn a veil over the excitement. Charles X then shook hands all round and Mass was celebrated in the chapel at Holyrood by Father Gillis. The Kay text continues:

> When the service terminated, a great many ladies and gentlemen of fashion paid their respects to his Majesty, the Duc d'Angoulême and the young Duc de Bordeaux who was a great favourite. In the hall of the palace a large party were also in waiting, with all of whom the King shook hands and bade them adieu. On the outside, the palace-yard was filled with people, many of whom wore white favours; and when the royal exiles appeared in the courtyard, they were greeted with cheers and the waving of handkerchiefs. The royal party then drove to Newhaven, where an immense crowd had assembled.

There was a bodyguard formed by the Society of Newhaven Fishermen, keeping clear the entrance to the Chain Pier, 'which was crowded with a large assemblage of respectable persons'. From the Chain Pier the royal party and Colonel Macdonell, Father Gillis, John Robison and Dr Browne embarked on the *Dart* which conveyed them to the *United Kingdom.* The Scottish contingent did not leave the *United Kingdom* until she was under weigh:

> The distress of the King, and particularly of the Dauphin, at being obliged to quit a country to which they were so warmly attached, was in the highest degree affecting. The Duc de Bordeaux wept bitterly; and the Duc d'Angoulême, embracing Mr. Gillis *à la Française*, gave unrestrained scope to his overpowering emotions. The act of parting with one so beloved, whom he had known and distinguished in the salons of the Tuileries and St Cloud, long before his family had sought an asylum in the tenantless halls of Holyrood, quite overcame his fortitude, and excited feelings too powerful to be repressed.

It was a shabby end to the second exile. So thought the Duke of Wellington. In the same letter to John Wilson Croker the Duke continues,

> When he went, they treated him in a very scurvy manner. The Duchesse d'Angoulême, in London, was unnoticed, excepting by a private visit from the Queen. They did not even give her a Government yacht or steam-boat; or to the King one of King William's vessels to carry him away. Her Royal Highness went in a common passage boat to Rotterdam, and His Majesty in a trader to Hambourg. Yet I know, and they know that when the family came here, there was nothing about which King Louis-Philippe was more anxious than that they should be received and treated with respect and attention, and everything done to provide for their accommodation. This want of respect and attention to them, therefore, is to be attributed to an innate desire to court the radicals and to manifest contempt (however cowardly) for fallen greatness.

Twice more in the nineteenth century Britain was to provide a place of refuge for the rulers of France, Louis-Philippe in his turn, after the uprising of 1848, and his successor, Napoleon III, in 1871, following on the defeat of France by Prussia at Sedan, both sought refuge in England. Their charitable and ready reception by the British Government only serves to underline the truth of the Duke of Wellington's assessment.

Epilogue: The Final Phase—Death of Charles in 1836

Four more years remained to Charles X. By way of Hamburg and Vienna the travellers reached Prague at the end of October 1832. There the Emperor Francis II put at their disposal a floor of the Hradschin Palace. In his rooms overlooking the old town, or at Butischirad, outside the city, where he passed the summer months, the ageing king witnessed the last convulsions of legitimacy.

The king was still en route for Prague when the news arrived of the arrest of Marie-Caroline, the Duchesse de Berry, at Nantes, where, betrayed by a double-agent called Deutz, she was discovered, black with soot, behind a fireplace of the house where she had been hiding. Undignified as this was, the royalist cause was further shattered by the announcement that the Duchesse had, on 10 May 1833, given birth to a child. The father, she maintained, was an Italian nobleman, the Count of Lucchesi-Palli to whom she had been secretly married on 14 December 1831 at Massa di Carrara. The marriage certificate is almost certainly a forgery, but in any case it has little to do with the paternity of the child unless one is prepared to believe that Lucchesi-Palli had, in the autumn of 1832, made the journey from the Hague, where he was serving as a diplomat, to closely guarded Nantes, without anyone having been aware of the fact.

Charles X found her conduct hard to bear since it revived old murmuring about the parentage of the Duc de Bordeaux. It was only with the greatest difficulty, when Marie-Caroline had been released by Louis-Philippe to whom, as his niece by marriage, she was an equal embarrassment, that Charles X could be persuaded to receive her. 'Let her,' he said, 'go to Palermo and live there with M. Lucchesi as his wife in the eyes of all the world; only then can one tell the children that their mother is married and may she come to embrace them.'

Thanks to the good offices of Chateaubriand, who had taken up her cause, the Duchesse de Berry was eventually allowed to see her children. Even then protocol forbade Charles to greet her at Hradschin, and the encounter took place at Loeben, outside Prague. This in turn gave rise to a characteristic scene with Marie-Caroline demanding that the King should receive her at Prague and Madame Royale being compelled to have the doors and windows shut to prevent half Bohemia hearing the complaints.

At this final phase of his life Charles X was, once more, to be at the centre of intrigue and to some extent its victim. The Duc de Bordeaux had come of age, having attained his fourteenth birthday, but the problem of his education and that of his sister remained fraught. At the heart of it all was the Baron de Damas, more intransigently illiberal as each year passed. In the end it was the Baron de Damas and two Jesuit priests whom he had imported who were ordered to leave. Another sadness was the dismissal of Madame de Gontaut, who was suspected of favouring a marriage between Princess Louise and one of the Orleans princes. One by one the Versailles faces were disappearing, but as he approached his eightieth year Charles X may have felt the gap narrowing between past and present. One moment, in particular, must have closed that gap—a moment when sentiment and shared memory could be given full rein. In May 1835, Stéphanie de Lage, 'Blimonette', visited Toeplitz, where the royal family were taking the waters. For weeks on end she and the king walked and sat recalling persons and places they had known more than half a century before. To her, and to her alone, he could talk of Louise de Polastron.

Life at Prague followed much the same routine as at Holyrood. From his set hour of rising, the morning Mass, the afternoon of reading or taking the air, dinner at six and whist at eight, to bed at precisely ten-thirty, the day was given a semblance of activity, and, it may be hoped that, with Charles's ability to live for the present, the semblance was for him a reality.

Unkind fate had not finished with him, however. The Emperor Francis II died at the end of 1835 and the coronation celebrations of his successor, Ferdinand I, were to take place in Prague the following summer. The palace of 400 rooms was not large enough to contain them both, and Charles X was told to move. On 26 May 1836 he left for Toeplitz, where, for the last time, he was to have the pleasure of the company of Madame de Lage.

'*Au revoir, sire,*' she said on parting. '*A l'année prochaine.*' '*Oui, à revoir*' he replied, '*à revoir, si . . .*'

Cholera was raging in upper Austria as the exiles moved south and the disease followed them. Goritz, now Goritzia, on the frontier between Italy and Slovenia, was reputed safe and Charles X arrived there in good health on 21 October. It was a mild autumn and the ex-king found his surroundings congenial in the little chateau of Graffenberg, overlooking the town.

On 3 November he became ill and cholera was diagnosed. Forty years exactly after he had arrived at Holyrood as a young *curé* who knew his place, the Cardinal de Latil administered the last rites, and on 6 November 1836 died the last King of France and Navarre. The Franciscan Monastery of Castagnavizza lies in what is now Slovenian territory. There Charles X was buried in the family vault of the Counts of Thurn. The doors have the family crest, which, by a strange co-incidence, incorporates two sceptres set with fleurs-de-lis.

Seven hundred miles away, in France, the Paris to St Germain railway was about to open for passenger traffic, and Parisians were to enjoy the experience of covering eighteen kilometres in twenty-nine minutes. Balzac had published *Père Goriot* and Madame Tussaud had opened, in London, her waxworks of the French Revolution. A watershed had been crossed.

Sources and Bibliography

Manuscript Sources

Except where otherwise indicated in the text, the relevant English language material is in the following: Public Record Office, State Papers Domestic, series H.O. 102, particularly H.O. 102/13. Scottish Record Office, Exchequer, Declared Accounts, Auditor 1795–1801 etc; Exchequer Letter Book, E 310 *et seq.*

The Trotter accounts are in Edinburgh University Library, Laing MS, II 499/29. The 'weighing' at Dalkeith Palace is in the Library Records, NLS, MS Acc.6248(8). I am indebted to Margaret Swain for this reference. The Arniston House reference (a private archive) is Vol. VII. The correspondence between Angoulême and the Duchess of Buccleuch is in the Buccleuch archives.

The principal French manuscript source is in the French Foreign Office, *Archives des Affaires Etrangères, Fonds Bourbons*, Vol. 626 and following volumes.

The de Boisgelin diaries are in the Bibliothèque Méjane, Aix-en-Provence, reference MS 1318–1329. (former reference 1191–1202).

Some extracts from the de Boisgelin diary have been printed in the *Book of the Old Edinburgh Club*, Vol. 28, p. 191, but the translations have been revised.

Printed Sources

General

My starting point has been A. Francis Steuart, *The Exiled Bourbons in Scotland*, Edinburgh,1908, but the citations have been checked. For the life and times of Artois I have used the following biographies: J. Lucas-Dubreton, *Le Comte d'Artois, Charles X*, Paris, 1927: Jaques Vivent, *Charles X—Dernier Roi de France et Navarre*, Paris 1958; Jean-Paul Garnier, *Charles X—Le Roi et le Proscrit*, Paris, 1967: André Castelot, *Charles X*, Paris, 1988; Georges Bordenove, *Charles X*, Paris, 1990. For Louise de Polastron: Vicomte de Reiset, *Louise d'Esparbes, Comtesse de*

Polastron, Paris, 1907; Monique de Heurtas, *Louise de Polastron*, Paris, 1983; Also, Phillipe Lauzun, *Un Portrait de Madame de Polastron*, Auch, 1906, and Comtesse de Reinach-Foussemagne, *Madame de Polastron d'après une Correspondence Inedite*, Paris, 1907.

The letters exchanged between Artois and the Comte de Vaudreuil have also been a major source; Léonce Pingaud, *Correspondence Intime du comte de Vaudreuil et du comte d'Artois pendant l'Emigration (1789–1815)*, 2 vols., Paris, 1889.

Particular Quotations will be found in:

Ainslie, Sir Philip Barrington, (Philo Scotus) *Reminiscences of a Scottish Gentleman*, London, 1861

Anon. *The Hermit in Edinburgh; or Sketches of Manners*, etc., 3 vols., London, 1824

Arnot, Hugo, *History of Edinburgh*, 2nd edn, Edinburgh, 1788

Boigne, Comtesse de, *Mémoires de la Comtesse de Boigne*, 2 vols., Paris, 1979; also, partial English translation, 2 vols., London, 1907

Castelot, André, *La Duchesse de Berry*, Paris, 1963

Castries, Duc de, *La Vie Quotidienne des Émigrés*, Paris, 1966

Castries, Duc de, *Les Émigrés*, Paris, 1962

Chambers, Robert, *Traditions of Edinburgh*, 2 vols., Edinburgh, 1825

Cobban, Alfred, *A History of Modern France*, Vol. 2, 2nd edn., London, 1965

Courtoy, Henry, *Historical Guide to the Abbey and Palace of Holyrood*, Edinburgh. Quotations are from the second edition of 1838

Damas, Baron de, *Mémoires du baron de Damas*, (1785–1862), 2 vols, Paris, 1923

Davies, Lady Clementina, *Recollections of Society in France and England*, 2 vols., London, 1872

Diesbach, Ghislain, *Histoire de l'Emigration*, Paris, 1975

Dibdin, James C., *Annals of the Edinburgh Stage*, Edinburgh, 1888

Gontaut, Duchesse de, *Mémoires de Madame la Duchesse de Gontaut*,

Gouvernante des Enfants de France pendant la Restauration, 1773–1823, Paris, 1891

Grant, Elizabeth, of Rothiemurchus, *Memoirs of a Highland Lady*, 2 vols, Edinburgh, 1988 (The most complete version)

Grant, Anne, of Laggan, *Memoir and Correspondence of Mrs. Grant of Laggan*, 3 vols., London, 1844

Gordon, Pryse Lockhart, *Personal Memoirs and Reminiscences*, 2 vols., London, 1830

Halkerston, Peter, *Treatise on the History, Law and Privileges of the Palace and Sanctuary of Holyroodhouse*, Edinburgh, 1831

Kay, John, *Edinburgh Portraits*. The re-issue of 1877 has been used.

Lockhart, John Gibson, *Life of Sir Walter Scott*, Edinburgh edn, 1903, vol. IX.

Maclean, James, and Skinner, Basil, *The Royal Visit of 1822*, Edinburgh, 1972

Mackenzie Stuart, A.J., *A Royal Debtor at Holyrood*, Stair Society, vol. 26, (1971) p.193; *The Lord Advocate and the French Spy*, Scots Law Times, 7 December 1979

Michel, Francisque, *Les Ecossais en France* etc, vol. 2, London, 1862

Montlosier, Comte de, *Souvenirs d'un Emigré*, Paris, 1951

Nettement, Alfred, *Mémoires Historiques de S.A.R. Madame Duchesse de Berry*, 3 vols., Paris, 1837

Omond, George W.T., *The Lord Advocates of Scotland*, 2 vols., Edinburgh, 1883

Portalis, Baron, *Henri-Pierre Danloux et son Journal pendant l'Emigration*, Paris, 1910

Reinach-Foussemagne, Comtesse de, *La Marquise de Lage de Volude*, Paris, 1908

Ross, Walter, *Lectures on Conveyancing*, 1st edn, Edinburgh, 1792

Sèze, Romain de, *Souvenirs d'Holyrood*, Paris, 1831

Sèze, Romain de, *Nouveau Souvenirs d'Holyrood*, Paris, 1832

Stuart, Lady Louisa, *Gleanings from an Old Portfolio*, Privately printed, 1895

Stuart, Lady Louisa, *Letters to Miss Louis Clinton*, Edinburgh, 1901

Summerson, John. *Architecture in Britain, 1530–1830*, London, 1953

Swain, Margaret, *Furniture for the French Princes at Holyrood, The Connoisseur*, January, 1978.

Weiner, Marjorie, *The French Exiles*, John Murray, London, 1960